Living with the Dragon

the Dragon

Healing 15 000 days of Abuse and Shame

JASON LEE

Tellwell Talent
www.tellwell.ca

ISBN
978-1-77370-171-4 (Hardcover)
978-1-77370-170-7 (Paperback)
978-1-77370-172-1 (eBook)

Table of Contents

Acknowledgements

There are so many people to thank for making this book possible. I'd like to thank and honour all those who have played such a valuable part in my life and inspired me to write this book.

First, I would like to acknowledge my father, Anthony, who passed away in 2010. He left us the day before I got offered my job and I still remember the rollercoaster of feelings from sadness and grief to confusion and excitement about my new job. I'd like to think it was a gift from him from above. My dad raised me as best he knew how and despite the suffering and pain, I still very much thank him for the life we had. Without him, none of what I've learned about myself and my journey would be possible. I truly believe the hardships were a lesson to be learned with a greater purpose. Thank you, Dad, and may you rest in peace.

I am also grateful to my mom, Mary, who not only did her best to raise three kids alongside my dad, she's never given up on me. Despite a lot of sadness and grief in our lives and the walls that I build, you have never stopped trying to reach me.

To Joshua, my beautiful and brave son: thank you for being my light, my love, and my best friend. You are wise beyond your years, yet your youth brings so much energy into my life and motivates me every single day to strive to be a better father and friend to you. May this book help you know me more and also help you discover a part of yourself. Enjoy life, my friend, and live it to the most because you know someday, "The Apes will be coming!"

I would like to thank Pearlynne, my ex-wife and my soul mate. I say this proudly and know that this journey couldn't have been possible without you. You are my guide, my lifeline, and my dear friend. I admire your strength and courage to face what you have endured in your journey. I wish you a world of success, happiness, and love.

Connie and Baxter: you are my beloved bunnies and your happy greetings bring me immediate smiles when I come see you.

To my newest love, Inori the cat. I knew I had to adopt you when I saw you through that window.

A very special acknowledgement to Guillermo Comesana and Anita Bloy, my two therapists with whom I worked the most. I truly believe your work and effort went beyond what is required for your profession and I felt your hearts reaching out to me. Thank you for listening, and for your work, wisdom, validation, and gentle guidance. When you are at the end of your careers, I hope you can be proud to say you truly made a difference in this man's life.

I am grateful to my friends for the many ways they have supported me. Christine - you are by far the most compassionate person I know. Your concern for others is a beautiful and rare gift. Catherine – thank-you for listening without judgement during some challenging days. Your commitment to God inspires me. Joanne - your strength on your spiritual journey has guided me with hope. Vincent - you're like the younger brother I never had. You're an awesome friend with so much energy and passion. Alex, Lynnessa, Randy, Rene, and Michelle – you've been my posse for decades and my friends that simply know how to be silly and have a good time!

And finally, I'd like to thank Lisa for opening my world to healing. You were my light, my love, my pain, and my sweetest friend. May you find stillness, peace, courage, and love on your life journey.

This book is dedicated to the "J"s in my life.

Preface

*It would be a terrible mistake to go
through life thinking that people are
the sum total of what you see.*

– Jonathan Tropper

Who is this guy named Jason Lee who decided to write a book? Allow me to introduce myself. Let me begin by saying I'm not a therapist, healer, nor a doctor by any stretch. I'm not a celebrity or a politician. I'm not on TV commercials or even on infomercials for that matter. I'm not the guy sitting along the sidewalk asking for money, nor am I someone who wanders along the streets of Vancouver looking for a fix. I'm just an average Canadian-born Chinese male in my forties. I hold a great job that allows me to travel often. I live in a modest apartment in the suburbs, pay taxes, have a teenage son, was married once, enjoy watching hockey, like exercising, love junk food, and dislike traffic. Yes, I'm the guy you see at the supermarket buying his weekly supply of milk, eggs, and toiletries who you probably didn't take much notice of.

Much like you, I'm just an everyday citizen who works hard and simply wants to enjoy life.

However, a month after my 42nd birthday, a hard reality hit me. I've always known myself as a few things: I'm passionate, romantic, thoughtful, considerate, easy going, stubborn, and hot headed at times...wait a second...did I say hot headed? Instead of the relaxed and easy-going guy I believed I was, I suddenly realized I was actually an angry, depressed, insecure, and resentful individual. I realized I was suppressing these feelings and wearing a mask to pretend life was working out wonderfully. How is it even possible to discover I am a completely different person from who I thought I was? How did I become all this?

After returning from a business trip in April, 2015, and after another string of arguments about my abusive behaviour towards her, my fiancée moved out.

"What a load of bullshit!" I thought in my enraged state.

"I made it this far in life with great friends, a great job, and a great kid. Who's she to say shit like that about me?"

Later in quiet solitude, it finally hit me. What if she was right? What if the person who truly loved me was telling the truth based on what she saw? After all, she did love me very much, so why would she say something to intentionally hurt me?

I stopped for a few moments to consider the ounce of possibility that she was right. I took that opportunity to challenge myself to take accountability. In the late hours one Saturday night, I searched the internet and read up on abuse. In a frightfully eye-opening moment, I finally realized who I was. Instead of turning my feelings outward with blame, I chose to shift my thoughts inward and learned to accept, embrace, and openly share about the abuse and shame I had put on my loved ones.

In this book, I share how I am managing to turn my life around. With the help of tools I discovered, I have lifted myself above the dark clouds and have started an enlightening and inspiring journey of healing and understanding.

This book starts with my childhood and teenage years growing up in an abusive home with an older brother with a mental illness. This set the stage for me for years of undiagnosed depression, anxiety, and suppressed anger. This anger would eventually be taken out in adulthood on all those who were ever close to me. However, in the public eye, I was just the guy lining up at the supermarket smiling, buying a loaf of bread, and wishing everyone I met a nice day. I take you through the difficulties I faced coping with anger, anxiety, and depression, and how I began to shift my life in a positive direction.

Alarmingly, one third of Canadian adults have suffered from some form of child abuse.[1] Many of us suffer quietly alone as adults and bury the shame deep inside us. It is often the root source of many of our daily struggles and can affect us unknowingly. It affects how we conduct ourselves in our relationships with our partners, family members, work colleagues, and friends. We often feel ashamed to acknowledge our past; it takes courage to talk about it. But until we do so in a healthy manner, our struggles will continue throughout our lifetime and will be passed along to our kids. The abuse has lifelong effects such as depression, anger, anxiety, fear, low self-esteem, and loneliness.

I decided to write this book for several reasons. For one, putting thoughts down on paper is cathartic. Sharing my story – one that I've hidden for decades - is liberating to me. I get to unlock and accept my past and allow my friends, family members, and other interested readers to know the real me.

Another reason for writing this book is to help others who are suffering from childhood abuse or have been abusive in their relationships. If this is you, I hope my story can speak to you so you know you're not alone. My goal is to pursue something greater in life: to inspire others and to share the tools I've used to get through my personal experiences and challenges with my inner health. I'm just an ordinary person who decided to make a change in his life by bravely taking a deep dive inside myself. After a couple of failed yet meaningful relationships and a son who's growing up to model after my behaviour, I realized that the only variable is me. We can all have challenges in our lives and that's okay, but it's how we manage our thoughts and behaviour and what we decide to do with them that matters. My shift in beliefs and values is something I hope readers will find inspiring and attainable.

Third, I wrote this book for the sake of accountability. Although my story might be inspiring to some, it does not take away the scars of those I have hurt. Sometimes apologies aren't enough. By sharing the poor choices and mistakes I've made, I hold myself to the highest accountability.

And lastly, I'm hoping by reading this, my son will gain a better understanding of himself and his journey in life.

Wherever your path started and wherever it has led you, I wish you all the best in your journey. Most of all I wish you continued courage and strength to face the truths within yourself for a healthier future. There is no greater feeling than liberation and being able to live your most honest self.

Introduction

In Chinese folklore, the dragon is a fiery, fierce creature symbolizing great strength and power. Its image, depicted in paintings and architecture and on vases and garments, is a sign of good luck, good fortune, and success because it was once the symbol that represented imperial power in ancient China. People described as having the personality of a dragon are known to be forthcoming, stubborn, and short-tempered, with a flaming tongue. They can be angry and enraged one moment and cunning and manipulative the next.

I believe there's a dragon living inside every one of us. I describe the dragon as the embodiment of suffering we have faced in our life. The dragon feeds and grows on our negative thoughts, beliefs, and unhappiness. It lives on our anxiety and depression, giving it strength to spit out fire in the form of anger, blame, resentment, and judgement of others. It can be relentless, merciless, cruel, and seemingly uncontrollable. Some dragons are much smaller than others and do very little harm. But for me, the dragon inside was larger than life. This is my story.

CHAPTER 1

The Dragon Rises: Childhood

"I didn't know that this was a Chinese restaurant!" mocked a party of Caucasians after we had a pleasant family dinner at the Copper Kettle.

When I was no more than 10 years old, my family went out for a Canadian buffet dinner with some family friends. We had just finished our meal when a group of middle-aged Caucasians arrogantly brushed by our table with their offensive remark. What I remember most were the roaring jeers from the other men and women in the party and the look of helplessness, shame, and loss of dignity in my parents' eyes as they tried their best to ignore the obviously discriminatory remark.

I am a second generation Asian male, born and raised in Vancouver, BC, Canada. I grew up in the 1970s and 80s when society was still adapting to Asians in the western world. Prejudice was prevalent. There were very few sushi restaurants, Chinese food was still considered foreign, and the language barrier sparked many discriminatory remarks from Westerners.

In the late 1980s to 90s, the mass immigration of families from Hong Kong into a society that was unprepared for change sparked further discrimination. With their different hairstyles, language, and popular culture, they were often the victims of ridicule, rage, and bullying in public schools.

I also remember being a regular target of racial slurs such as being called a "Chinaman" or "Chink" throughout my years in school. There was a blond-haired boy in elementary school who often teased me by imitating the Chinese language and saying things such as "welcome to Canada!" while pulling the ends of his eyes up with his fingers and squinting. One time, I stomped on the boy's foot and told him to shut up. One of the teachers saw what happened and pulled me aside and lectured me on how wrong I was to retaliate.

My parents came to Canada from Brunei in 1968. Where is Brunei, you ask? It's that tiny country on the northern part of the island of Borneo, near Malaysia and Singapore. As one can imagine, finding work in Canada as an Asian man or woman was difficult, even though both my parents were fluent in English. Moving to Canada, my parents had the challenging task of assimilating to a new culture and raising three kids in a Western society with beliefs much different than those in Asia. Growing up, we spoke part

Cantonese (Chinese) and part English, or, as some people say, "Chenglish."

Growing up, I was very fortunate to have many great things in my life. I always had a roof over my head, delicious meals cooked by my mom, and the necessities for childhood entertainment. We didn't go out for dinner often partly because my mom was an amazing cook but mostly because eating out was expensive for a working-class family.

Until I was 7 years old, we lived across the street from a park called Trout Lake. I have vague memories of walking in knee high snow and skating on the frozen lake during the winter months. In the summer, we would run across the field of grass and sometimes fly a kite. We had a swing set in our backyard and a big apple tree which I enjoyed climbing with my siblings. Our neighbours were delightful families who enjoyed teasing me. I would scowl back at them with my squeaky 4-year-old voice and say, "what's so funny?"

In our two-floored house in East Vancouver, my siblings and I shared a bedroom. I slept in a bed with my older brother, Joseph, while my older sister, Jackie, had a bed of her own. Often, I would sneak into my parent's room in the middle of the night because I had difficulty falling asleep. Within moments of being sandwiched between the two of them, I was quickly off to dreamland. My mom's younger brother, Stephen, lived downstairs and he worked part time at the local A&W to help the family. There was one bathroom upstairs for everyone to share. My dad eventually built an extra bathroom downstairs which we didn't end up using very much because it was poorly lit and musty. It was a crowded home, but one which we were quite fond of.

I was a very emotional child and often very vocal with opinions. I was outspoken with my family and their friends if I heard something I didn't agree with. I was short tempered, yet caring and sensitive. I especially loved animals like our pet turtle, Seek, and two rabbits, Snowy and Chewy. I looked after them with my sister and we made it a routine to feed the bunnies every day at 8 a.m. and 8 p.m. at night for the eight years they were with us. I often insisted that the rabbits should live inside our house and be allowed to roam freely like a pet dog, but naturally my parents would have nothing of it.

I was also a very creative child. I would go to the library and borrow books on how to paint, draw, craft, and create my own board games which I often did. I even once tried to build my own clock out of cardboard. The idea ended, however, after I realized my ambition and reality weren't in sync. Along with art class, I enjoyed creative writing throughout elementary school. I loved writing fictional stories about mysteries, dragons, and mighty kings. In fact, in grade 4, I loved it so much I wrote plays for the class to read and act out on a weekly basis during the final months of school. My teacher, Ms. Peterson, encouraged me and I ran with my passion. I did well in elementary school and was typically one of the top two students in my class in terms of grades. I was liked by all my teachers because of my studious and obedient behaviour.

At home it was a different story. There I was vocal and challenged authority. My mom would sometimes threaten to tell my teachers how belligerent I was at home because all my teachers thought I was a model student for behaviour. At home, I often found myself getting into trouble. Because I was opinionated and the youngest in the family, my ideas generally weren't very popular with the other four members. Having strong opinions in front of my dad was always a big mistake.

My Dad

My dad worked various jobs after starting in the lumber industry in central BC. By nature, my dad was often angry and irritable. I can only imagine the amount of prejudice he faced as a new immigrant in the late 1960's; perhaps this fueled some of his anger during times of stress and hardship. However, his anger ran deeper than that and began in his childhood and youth back in Brunei. It ran deep into an Asian culture that reinforced in him the value of being hard working, emotionally stoic, and disciplined.

Dad worked hard and looked after the house, garden, and bills. He was what you would call "the provider." From time to time, he would enjoy the occasional beer while watching TV, but he never abused alcohol in any way. He worked at BC Transit for over 15 years and received praise for his tenure and work ethic there. He certainly was a proud employee of BC Transit and worked hard every day, not wanting to miss work even when he was sick or injured.

My dad loved gardening and building little things in the yard. He even built the houses for our pet rabbits which had multiple stories and fancy swinging doors. He spent days carefully building their hutch with spare wood and chicken wire he had from the yard. He even insulated part of their home to keep them warm during the winter months. Measuring, sawing, and hammering away, I could see the delight in his face when the rabbits bounced inside their new mansion.

When I was in Grade 5 dad built me my first bike and taught me how to ride it. He found a spare bike frame from work and took pride in building it and showing me how neat the back-pedal brakes were. The bike also included one training wheel on the left side of the bike. The exception was that it was as large in size as the back wheel and made the bike look like it had a side car, minus the car part.

In his later years, he was very fond of his only grandson, Joshua (my son), and my ex-wife, Pearl. He always greeted them both with a warm smile.

My father passed away in 2010 on a September afternoon. I was picking up my son from school when my sister Jackie sent me a text to let me know that dad had just passed away. I remember feeling a little sad and mostly emotionally numb on getting the news. I remember feeling the world was quieter and emptier without him - as though I could hear a pin drop on the floor.

My relationship with my dad was regrettably never close. We never connected well from the time I was a child. He wasn't much of a talker. Even as adults when we tried to communicate, I never felt emotionally safe enough to share much with him. When I was a child he didn't show much emotion around me other than anger with a few blurred moments of love.

When I think back to his daily waves of anger and rage, I grieve for a man who lived his life in fear, shame, and resentment beneath the surface of what the outside world saw. Often, if he wasn't shouting or yelling at someone, he would still be giving off an aura of fear. We needed to be cognizant of him and make sure we didn't make too much noise to trigger him. We couldn't do the things that kids typically do like laugh and play without him getting agitated and angry.

Neighbourhood kids who rang the doorbell to ask if I wanted to come outside to play would get yelled at and lectured by him, and he would turn his rage towards me afterwards. He sometimes yelled at neighbourhood kids for walking on our lawn. One time he even went as far as yelling, "Shut up you retard!" to a young mentally challenged boy for saying hello to him on the front lawn.

We weren't allowed to have friends over because my parents feared they might steal something from the house. The only exceptions were kids of family friends, but we couldn't bring them upstairs into our rooms to play because my dad was paranoid they might snoop and pocket something during their visit.

When I was 4 years old I was given an awesome Big Loader construction site set for Christmas. It was a battery-operated construction site with motorized trucks hauling rocks around a plastic track. When word came that company was coming over, he told me to quickly put it away before Darren, the child of these family friends, would want to play with it and possibly break it.

I loved playing with Lego as a kid. One evening, Darren came over to play with his Lego spaceship with me. As boys do, we played, laughed, and had a good time. My dad returned home from work at 4 p.m. and was quieter and more withdrawn than he normally was. After my friend went home, my dad immediately turned to me and began raising his voice. He reamed me out, saying, "Why were you guys so loud?! Can't you see that I just got home from work?!" He continued to complain to my mom in the kitchen about our behaviour as I sat alone in the next room quietly listening to my dad verbally slam me for misbehaving.

My dad was often fixing the family car in the garage. The "green tank" as we referred to it was an old station wagon that took us everywhere, including Disneyland one summer. The outside of the vehicle was a solid piece of metal and I don't recall it ever getting a dent or scratch on it. As the years went by, my father spent more and more time repairing the engine. He worked hard fixing the car and was often frustrated, judging by the frown in his thick eyebrows and pursed lips after a long evening in the garage. One time I meekly offered him a glass of milk as a gesture to hopefully ease some of his frustration. He turned, looked at me with angry eyes, and screamed, "CAN'T YOU SEE THAT I'M BUSY?!" Without replying, I sheepishly tiptoed away with the glass of milk still in my hand, feeling rejected.

Growing up I was often told to be a "good boy" or "*guai-chai*" in Cantonese. I was no more than 4 years old and we had just finished our Happy Meals from McDonald's in the kitchen. We each had one and my sister and I were equally tempted by the colourful display of fun activities on the Happy Meal boxes. My brother, who is 7 years older, said he didn't want his Happy Meal box. On hearing this, my sister and I pounced on the opportunity to claim it. We fussed, whined, shouted, and cried until my dad stormed furiously into the kitchen, grabbed the cardboard box and crushed it into a ball right before our eyes. He tossed it into the garbage and shouted, "NO MORE MCDONALD'S FROM NOW ON!"

My mom sat there quietly and whispered to me: "that's what you get for not being a *guai-chai*."

Instead of teaching the values of sharing, kindness, and patience, my parents resorted to abuse, terror, and guilt to resolve conflicts. Fear and threats were commonly used tools to maintain order in our household. If these tactics didn't work, they used physical abuse.

One of my most painful memories is from a time when I was 7 years old and living in our new home in North Burnaby. My brother was conducting one of his regularly scheduled bullying sessions on me until we got into a fight. As always, he out-muscled me and I ended up screaming and wailing until my dad came storming in from the backyard.

My dad carried a two foot long piece of wood, about one inch thick. My body trembled with fear and my breaths became short and shallow when I heard the stomping steps on the sundeck. He ripped the sliding door open and without even asking what was going on, beat me to the ground with the stick. I was knocked to the floor and I wailed and screamed even louder. This fueled his rage even more and he continued to beat me with the stick. I writhed on the ground in pain while my brother stood there watching and my sister was frozen with helplessness. My pulsating cries begged him to stop, but Dad just yelled, "*mo-cho!*" in Cantonese, which means "shut up" or "quiet down", while continuing to beat me more into submission. The beating left bruises on the back of my leg and a limp that lasted for days.

He topped off the abuse by yelling at me for tracking dirt into the house with my dirty socks, of all things. He roared and ordered me to get out of the house to clean my socks. I desperately crawled outside like a crippled animal and sat on the sundeck crying in pain. Wiping away my tears, I desperately tried to rub the dirt off my white socks with only the sweat from my fingers. I sat there for what felt like hours, trembling helplessly and alone with my wounds.

Later that night when my mom returned home from work, she noticed the bruises on my leg, which took on the shape of the stick, and that I was hobbling like a wounded animal. She must have eventually found out what happened from my dad. When she spoke to me, she told me that this is what happens when I misbehave and that I should be a *guai-chai*.

One of my greatest fears of my dad was hearing his rapid foot-steps stomping towards me so he could give out one of his vicious blows. My heart would beat frantically, my chest would tighten, and I would whimper in fear on the floor even before he showed up. And when he finally did, the vicious beatings accompanied by his roaring rage left a lasting pain.

· · · · ·

During Christmas, I eagerly looked forward to all the cartoon specials that would be aired on TV. Every Friday when we got the new TV Guide, I circled all the programs I wanted to watch and excitedly told my sister about them. We didn't have a VCR at the time and only had the one television which we affectionately called "Bang-Bang." We named it "Bang-Bang" because you literally had to bang the top of the TV really hard repeatedly to get the colour back. I was notorious for waking up the entire house at 7 a.m. on Saturday mornings watching the Smurfs and aggravatingly banging away at the TV to bring the blue back into those Smurfs.

On one particular weeknight during the Christmas season when I was 9 years old, my dad was watching his favourite war documentary on TV. I was feeling anxious that I was going to miss my Christmas special on CBS because it was only minutes before the start of the show. My dad continued to watch his show and it was already five minutes past the start time of the cartoon that I was dying to watch. I pleaded to my dad to let me watch my special and he blatantly ignored me. I continued to plead and whine until he got so irate he flipped the channel to the cartoon. He then stood up from the couch, stared me down, and reached over to grip my nose with his fingers and began twisting it like a vice. He sneered, "You go ahead and watch your stupid show!" before storming out of the room.

My dad had very little tolerance for noise in the house whether it was the sound of pop music, laughter, or arguments. There was a rare time when my brother, sister, and I played a board game together when we were in our teens. The board game was called Risk and the goal of the game was world domination. The game contained some dice, a stack of cards and about 50 coloured plastic pieces that represented each of our armies. On one occasion my brother and I were on the brink of losing the game to my sister. My brother started getting agitated and began harassing her with name-calling and put-downs. She yelled back and told him to stop but his anger overtook him and he stood up and started shoving her. She screamed and began to shove back, refusing to concede to his abuse. The two of them continued to argue and shove each other until we heard the gallop of my dad's footsteps from upstairs. He stormed into the kitchen with fire in his eyes. In one foul-swoop he knocked the board game and all its tiny plastic pieces to the floor. The three of us watched in horror - terrified and frozen. My dad looked at my brother and roared, "I TOLD YOU NOT TO PLAY THIS STUPID GAME!" He continued yelling at the three of us and started cursing as we immediately scrambled to the floor to pick up the pieces. Terrified, we never again brought out that game.

My father even once went so far as to strike his 3-year-old nephew visiting with my aunt from Brunei. We were at the shopping center and dad was left alone attending my cousin at the mall's play area for kids while the rest of us wandered around the mall for no more than half an hour. My cousin was a curious 3-year-old by nature and had a lot of energy to burn off; this proved to be overwhelming for my dad. When the rest of the family returned to the play area, we saw the boy run to his mom crying profusely with a bleeding lip. The story my dad told to my mom later that evening was that my cousin was misbehaving and climbed somewhere he wasn't supposed to and fell down. The boy's crying enraged my dad, and so he slapped my cousin in the face. My dad went on arguing and justifying his actions by saying that he was disobedient and needed to be slapped. It was unclear whether the bloody lip resulted from the fall or from the slap. My mom later explained to my dad, "You can't hit other people's kids! It's a different story if it's your own kid..."

Based on Chinese culture and beliefs, from what I've observed in the families I knew growing up, it isn't unusual for parents to use sticks, belts, or bamboo sticks (from feather dusters) to beat their kids. Paired with a good dose of yelling, lectures, put-downs, and guilt whenever their kids disobey by failing to practice piano, go to Chinese school, or get straight As, this creates a classic formula for the traditional Asian hierarchy.

As adults, my sister has been resolute about the traditional Asian methods and seems to dismiss the past by saying, "It wasn't that bad" or "all of us went through it" whenever the topic of abuse has come up. As long as we continue to deny the pain, we will unknowingly pass on those beliefs and traditions to future generations.

I said goodbye to my dad for the last time in September, 2010 on a cloudy afternoon. It is unfortunate that we didn't have the capacity to build a relationship later in life. It simply hurt too much for me to open that door. I stopped having worthwhile conversations with him after my divorce in 2001. I separated myself from the family during this period with only the occasional visit during holiday dinners.

· · · · ·

In April, 2015 when I was 42 years old, I recall sitting cross-legged in my bedroom alone. I remembered an exercise I had learned from the book *Becoming the Kind Father*.[2] My eyes were closed and I had a gentle image of my dad listening quietly to me. I finally thanked him for doing his best, acknowledged his efforts in raising me the best he knew how, and said a proper and peaceful goodbye to him. I tearfully told him that I no longer wanted to carry the weight of the abuse and shame. I explained calmly and with conviction that I didn't need him anymore. I told him I am worthy and lovable despite what he made me believe with his abuse. Then I opened my eyes, and he was gone. I stood up, dried my eyes, grabbed my cap, and went out for a walk. The sun shone on my face and I felt uplifted and prepared to move forward, now free from the burden of his beliefs.

My brother - the early years

Regrettably my relationship with my older brother, Joseph, didn't have the opportunity to develop into anything lasting. He is seven years older than me and by the time I was around 14 years old he went away to the University of Western Ontario. He came back only at Christmas and for the summers. I started to miss him when he was away because in the few years previous to him leaving I was maturing into someone who was starting to connect with him; there was somewhat of a brotherly relationship developing since we didn't fight as often. I remember he even took me to a few movies downtown. Afterwards we would drive around Stanley Park listening to some New Order and OMD on the cassette deck. During those years I was starting to look up to him as my big brother and felt cool that I was hanging out with someone from university.

However, that relationship was short-lived. Sadly, he fell into a mental illness and started to show signs of it by the time I was 16 years old. Our relationship began to crumble with arguments and fights that were much different than when we were just boys. I wasn't able to connect with him and my lack of compassion and understanding of his challenges made it even more difficult. We eventually stopped talking to each other and I no longer felt comfortable even being in the same room as him, fearing another argument would break out. A few years later he was diagnosed with acute schizophrenia.

In earlier years, I don't recall many occasions of us spending time together. There are two fond memories that do come to mind. Back in East Vancouver where I spent my first 7 years, I remember playing softball with him and Jackie in the backyard. I was only about 4 at the time and I remember always hitting a "home run" with the plastic ball over the roof of our detached garage. He would have to run to get the ball in an uncomfortable space between the garage and the neighbour's fence and I would find amusement in my somewhat deliberate actions.

My second memory is one that I sometimes forget but should not take for granted. He taught me how to play hockey. We played downstairs and I would always be goalie; this was likely what got me interested in playing goal in ball hockey leagues in my later years, which I truly enjoyed. I remember one time I accidentally high-sticked him between his eyes and drew quite a bit of blood which trickled down his face. Despite this incident, he enjoyed playing with me, I think. Even when we moved to Burnaby we would play hockey downstairs quite a bit. He would take slap shots on me and I would pretend I was Richard Brodeur, Mike Palmateer or Rogie Vachon. Although these are very fond memories, I don't have many more that I can recall.

Joseph was a complicated person that I never quite understood nor truly felt a connection with. On one hand, he was my brother who taught me about the butterfly save. On the other hand, he was one of my greatest tormentors growing up. I don't mean teasing in a brotherly way, but a tormentor and bully. He would say things to get a rise out of me which initiated many of our fights which led to a lot of beatings by my dad. He wasn't the type of older brother who was proud to protect his kid brother. In fact, it was quite the opposite. He felt I was too much of a "sissy" to spend time with or to walk with to school. The put-downs and fights hurt me emotionally and physically. The most painful part, though, was the feeling that I couldn't look to my older brother for support.

We took a bus to the mall one time when I was around 8 years old. Admittedly, I had no sense of fashion and I was wearing my pants well above my ankles. As we disembarked the bus, some teenage girls mocked me by shouting, "floods-over!" which was slang used when people's pants were too short. My brother snickered and smirked. Although the remark from the girls was hurtful, the worst part was that my brother laughed with them. When we got home he enthusiastically shared the story with my parents and burst out laughing and continued teasing. My pride was injured and a fight ensued, followed by the routine beating from my dad.

I was often teased by my brother for being a boney and scrawny kid. We would get into wrestling bouts and fights that involved punching, pinching, yelling, shouting, and screaming. He outmuscled me every time and I would be pushed to the floor, crying and wishing someone would put an end to the torment.

He didn't appear interested in what was going on in my world except to make things difficult. I used to listen to old cassette tapes made by my Uncle Stephen of REO Speedwagon and the Powder Blues. My dad was strongly against us listening to rock or pop music. My brother would catch me listening to this tape from time to time and threaten to tell my dad. It was then the same routine:

I would get scared and feverishly fight back to get him to stop, we would push and shove and I would cry until dad beat me with the weapon of his choice, and my brother would simply be told to go to his room.

I sometimes look back on those years when my brother's mental health was declining and wish he had the love, attention, and compassion that he needed from me and the rest of the family. In a household filled with abuse and shame, there simply wasn't *space* for that, unfortunately. I think there would have been much more hope for him in his later years when he was truly suffering if he had received the love and care he needed from his family earlier.

My only contact with him now is extremely rare and brief. It's only been in the last few years that I have been brave enough to openly share with my friends and colleagues about his mental illness. I owe him that at the very least and it's a big start for me. I think of him now with true heartfelt compassion, guilt, regret, and love. I only wish that my courage would overcome my pain and allow me to reach out to him.

Being bullied

I started being bullied when I went to high school. The meanest bullies were two boys named Jeff and John who were conveniently placed in my classes throughout my high school years. Jeff was a boy who had a naturally mean look on his face with what seemed like a permanent scowl. He had short blond hair and a freckled face and would stand right up to my face challenging me to a fight for no reason. Face to face threats from Jeff and getting pushed to the ground by him used to frighten me the most.

"You Chinks are so fuckin' ugly," he would say staring me down and, "Get out of my face, you fuck'n' Chink!"

Jeff and John would laugh, ridicule, and tease me for how I looked, dressed, and for being meek. They were a fearsome pair and I did everything I could to avoid them. I would plan my way around them in the hallways and look at the floor as I walked to avoid eye contact. Teachers and staff weren't helpful and dismissed their behaviour even though it was brought to their attention. I felt completely helpless and thought my only option was to ride out my high school days suffering in solitude.

One time during career day, we had someone from the Canadian Armed Forces come speak to us. As I walked into the room a jock from the senior basketball team shouted: "Get out of here! Our country doesn't want you serving us!" The entire class burst out with mocking laughter as I awkwardly sat at my desk.

I didn't tell anyone at home because talking wasn't encouraged in my family. We were taught not to tell anyone our problems, again a common theme in Asian culture, as it was seen as shameful to demonstrate weakness. I would keep this all to myself and not a single family member knew about the bullying. It's only been in recent years that I have been able to speak openly about the experiences.

My former fiancée once said the reason I was bullied so much in school was because my dad took away a lot of my courage and self-esteem with the abuse. Therefore, bullies at school could see that fear in me and took advantage of my meek and weak personality. It took me a while to fully understand what she meant but the more I learned about abuse, the more I understood how shame strips away our self-worth. Without self-worth, my lack of confidence showed, making me a prime target for bullies.

My uncle

Growing up, one of my uncles (*"Cow-Fu"* or *"Ah-Cow"* as we used to call him in Cantonese), lived in Toronto. He was a younger brother to my mom. He and my mom spoke endlessly on the phone almost daily after 8 p.m. PST when it was cheaper to make long distance calls. They were very close and had a great relationship. In 1999 he passed away suddenly from a heart attack and I think my mom was never the same again. She misses that family bond that she doesn't share with any of her other siblings.

Ah-cow was the head of his family and led through harsh words, by instilling fear and shame, and with a fist. His two daughters had to play the piano, had to take Cantonese lessons, and of course, had to get good grades or there would be consequences. Oddly, his family was one I looked up to growing up. I'm not sure why, but whenever he and my aunt came to Vancouver to visit, my sister and I would be over the moon dancing happily that they would be coming with our two cousins. I recall wanting to be like him and his family: to have a nice home, a good job, to be a "leader" in the family and to have obedient kids who were flawless in every way.

Only recently did I realize that *Ah-Cow* was one of my most dominant original abusers. In fact, in a conversation I had with one of my counsellors, we identified that he was arguably one of the most dangerous of my abusers because his abuse went unknown and unidentified for so long. Whenever he called and I happened to pick up the phone, the conversations would steer in a direction of him yelling at me. He would intimidate and call me useless and lazy at home and accuse me of not doing anything worthwhile with my time.

One year, my sister and I spent the summer with *Ah-Cow's* family in Toronto. Staying at his home was like walking on eggshells. I was afraid of saying or doing anything that would trigger him to say something hurtful to me. One time while driving, he told my aunt in Cantonese about how bad I was and that they should drop me off at a juvenile hall.

One evening I was sitting on the couch watching TV. He walked over, sat down beside me, and ripped the remote control from my hand. He stared me down and flipped the channel to his Chinese program, roaring the words, "MY TV!" I didn't do anything except sheepishly walk away.

Many years later, *Ah-cow* was arrested for child abuse after he took a pair of scissors and cut a piece of hair off my cousin's head as punishment when they were running late for school. He was arrested, detained overnight, and removed from his family even though my aunt and cousins pleaded for his release so he could come back home. At the time our families argued that the judicial system was flawed and terribly wrong. When I look back I cringe at those beliefs and admit that *we* couldn't have been more wrong. He was an abusive man and unfortunately he wasn't brave enough to see that in himself as he criticized the judicial system even after his sentence was completed.

My aunt's attitude was not a whole lot different and she often looked at me with disdain. During that same summer, my sister and I sometimes got into arguments. We used to call each other names and a fight would break out which included a lot of screaming, pinching, and shoving. She once kept teasing me and continuously called me names. I wept quietly alone in the living room when my aunt came along and coldly asked, "What are you doing?"

I replied meekly, "Jackie keeps calling me Gopher..."

My aunt sneered, "Well, if you're going to cry, don't cry on my sofa!" and walked off carrying on with her business.

It's so important for us to identify and process all our abusers.[3] Often, these are the people whom we loved, trusted, followed, and relied on for guidance (such as our parents, caregivers, aunts, and uncles). I looked up to *Ah-cow* and my aunt while I was growing up and well into my thirties. I unknowingly worshipped their success and wanted to be much like them.

The most frightening part was that I once modelled my beliefs and values after their abusive behaviour. Their words and looks were harsh, guilt-inducing, and controlling and I mimicked this in my adult life believing it was a healthy and strong way to raise a family. Identifying all my abusers was an incredibly powerful tool in my healing process. It has helped me understand and put into context some of the actions and behaviour for which I am ultimately responsible.

Equally as important, I needed to move forward and no longer be a victim of their abuse. There were reasons behind their behaviour likely linked to their childhood. To accept that point is sometimes enough. Once we can accept that, we can begin to see that their actions were not a reflection of us and our self-worth. Like my counsellor, Anita, once explained to me, "sometimes we can't understand everything that happens, but we can accept it."

Difficult transitions

My family moved from a two-floor house in Vancouver's East 19th to a much bigger and brand new three-floor house in North Burnaby when I was part way through Grade 1. Although I was excited to be living in a much larger sized home and yard, I didn't realize the upcoming social challenges I would quickly face. Back in Vancouver my best friend was a girl named Anna whose mom used to babysit me while my mom was working. I also used to play in the school yard with two girls, Amy and Susan, and a boy named Galton. He was the first friend I remember phoning. The phone conversation was quite cute when I look back on it because it probably lasted no more than 60 seconds and was filled with nervous blank air space from a couple of 7-year-old boys.

"Hi...so, do you still live in the same house with the fence?" I asked not knowing what else to say.

"I didn't want to talk to you, did you?....ok, bye..."

When I got off the phone, Joseph, who was eavesdropping on the conversation, burst into a mocking laugh. "That was so stupid! I can't believe you don't know how to talk on the phone! So stupid!" He repeatedly taunted me regardless of my screeching and crying pleas to stop. My dad stepped in and followed up with a severe scolding and beating to stop me from crying.

Going to a new school in Grade 1 was perhaps one of the most challenging things I faced in my childhood. I was a shy kid and I just couldn't blend in well and socialize with any of the other children. I was particularly nervous around a boy named Kelly because of how chatty and popular he was in class and the fact that he sometimes taunted me. He also happened to be friends with the neighbours' kids who I was also terrified of even though they were around the same age as me. My dad and mom used to say that the neighbours' kids were terribly loud whenever they played in their backyard and "bad" kids because they ran through our yard and shouted a lot. (Ironically, Kelly and the neighbours' kids turned out to be some of my better friends from Grades 4 through 8. There's a lesson to be learned here that the fear likely stemmed from my own anxieties and social insecurities.)

Back in Grade 1, I spent my recess and lunch hours walking alone on wooden beams desperately waiting for the bell to ring. Occasionally I would see my sister Jackie, who was in Grade 4, do the same thing. I know that she had her struggles as well and I recall awkwardly talking to her in the schoolyard but not for very long as it wasn't socially acceptable for a Grade 4 girl to hang out with her little brother in Grade 1.

During this time I would cry at home almost every day and not want to go to school. One day my mom got so frustrated that she took me into school to talk to Ms. Brown. This teacher had a reputation for being a very mean person. Rumour had it that she still beat kids with rulers in 1980.

That day, Ms. Brown was equally frustrated so she singled me out, brought me up to the front of the classroom and asked the entire class, "Who here likes Jason?" Likely confused by the question, the other Grade 1 kids simply weren't sure how to answer it. I think a handful raised their hands and others simply didn't care about the question. I wasn't quite paying attention as I was making whining noises to my mom who was standing beside me. I was also looking shamefully down at the floor with my hands in my pockets until Ms. Brown yelled, "GET YOUR HANDS OUT OF YOUR POCKETS! YOU'RE A BIG BOY NOW!"

My mom

My mom worked extremely hard and was driven to work long hours to earn money. She used to work two jobs: one as a prep cook and the other in the kitchen at a hospital. She cooked dinner, did the laundry, ironed, knit, sewed, cleaned, and hosted big family dinners. She worked hard to provide a good meal every single day to a bunch of complaining family members. She would get up to go to work at 5 a.m. and get home sometimes not until 9 p.m. if she had a double shift. She didn't drive, so she often took the bus, walked, or had my dad pick her up. Very rarely would she ever sit down and watch TV unless it was one of her Chinese dramas that she enjoyed.

When I was young, I often craved her attention and would complain, "I'm bored."

Her go-to reply while she was preparing dinner was, "Jason! I'm busy. Can't you tell? Go read a book or find something else to do! Go bother someone else!"

When I was disobedient as a child, mom would resort to caning me with a bamboo stick or slap me in the face. One time when I was maybe 3 or 4 years old she tossed me out of the house as I cried endlessly for her to take me back. I stood bare foot on the front sidewalk screaming and crying for her and felt as though she didn't want me anymore. She eventually brought me back in the house, but not without scars.

On her days off she would be busy running errands, preparing meals or gardening, which meant that she spent very little time with any of the kids. She enjoyed grocery shopping in Chinatown and because she didn't drive, my dad would take her there after he picked her up from work at the hospital downtown. He was kind to her that way because he never complained about driving her places. However, her relationship with my dad wasn't one that displayed much love and affection (this tendency to hide affection is typical of most Asian parents).

My parents had many loud and frightening arguments that I could hear even from my upstairs bedroom. The rare quality time I remember them having together was at 4 p.m. after work when they would sit down for some tea and biscuits from Marks & Spencer that my mom enjoyed. They would usually chat about work and they would sometimes break into an argument even during this ritual they enjoyed. My mom would sometimes have very violent nightmares that even my dad would talk about in fear. I'm not sure, but they may have been related to the many tearful phone conversations she had with her relatives back in Brunei. Sadly, my mom lost many of her younger brothers over the years, mainly for health reasons. As the years have gone by I've noticed her smile and laughter slowly dissolve into invisibility.

More scars

Despite doing very well academically, most of my childhood memories involve a lot of shouting and fighting matches with my sister and brother. After the fights, I was often alone playing Lego or drawing in my room as a form of relief. During those times when I did get along with my sister, we would sometimes skip out from school to stay home and play school or house together. When I got to know the neighbourhood kids more, I would spend most of my after-school days playing street hockey.

When I was 9 years old, my sister, my mom, my uncle Stephen, and I went on vacation to Brunei and Singapore. I did not enjoy any part of this two month experience from start to finish. Throughout the better part of the trip, I fell ill. I was throwing up, not eating, feverish, and utterly exhausted. I must have been suffering from jet lag among other ailments and when my mom and uncle wanted to go out shopping and touring, I struggled to go out. My energy was low and my taste buds were off. Even McDonald's didn't taste right to me.

We were staying in a hotel in Singapore and one morning my mom, uncle, and sister were getting ready to head out for another tour. Family friends were coming shortly to pick us up from our room. I was feeling nauseous and feverish again and complained to my mom that I just wanted to stay in the hotel. I continued to whine while slowly getting undressed. My uncle, in an unexpected rage, beat me to the floor and began yelling at me to hurry up and get dressed. I screamed and wailed in pain, crying shamefully on the floor, wearing only my underwear at the time. The family friends arrived just at that moment and I remember my body lying halfway in the closet when I turned and saw images of all their faces staring down at me. I lay there feeling humiliated, ashamed, helpless, and completely unloved.

I was a sensitive child growing up and needed extra nurturing and attention - more than some other kids would. I was often told that I was overly emotional, too sensitive, and too outspoken. Many times, I felt as though I didn't fit into the family because I was by far the most vocal and opinionated of the three kids. My sister and brother did a much better job at conforming to the household rules. I was the first kid in our family to ever say, "Fuck you!" I was 7 years old and was trying to defend myself against my brother. Needless to say, I got a beating for that.

Growing up, our family didn't encourage conversations. I remember getting slapped in the face a few times at the dinner table for "talking nonsense" as they liked to put it. To be seen and not heard was a very common theme. The sharing of opinions, feelings, and thoughts was discouraged. Sometimes we were threatened by our parents and told to watch our tongue, or we'd get slapped, scolded, beaten, caned, or a combination of these. My dad would yell *"mo-cho!"* or *"Mo-gung-yeh!"* (which translate to, "shut up!" and "don't talk!") The beatings were done with their hands, a stick, a bamboo duster, a wooden ruler, or a belt.

· · · · ·

A healthy family experiences patience, compassion, love, listening, and understanding. Conflict will undoubtedly arise, however resolution in a healthy household begins with two-way communication rather than with arguments and attempts to have the loudest voice. I recently tried to have a conversation with my mom over dinner about what a healthy family looks like. I explained to her that what we had growing up was unhealthy and crippling in the long term. Unfortunately, the conversation was taken out of context, she took it personally as a failure on her part, and she got extremely defensive.

She began raising her voice and lecturing me: "Do you actually believe there are families out there that get along? Do you actually believe they don't argue and fight?"

I calmly replied, "Yes mom...there are families out there that truly get along. They sometimes argue and fight but they don't beat each other up or yell at the top of their lungs..."

Her eyes lit up with fire and she leaned in to me to say, "That's BULLSHIT! What a load of BULLSHIT!"

I disengaged and ended the conversation knowing that it was heading in the wrong direction. Although I don't know much about her growing up years, other than that she was the eldest daughter who looked after a dozen other siblings, I suspect that it wasn't an ideal childhood filled with love, compassion, and tolerance. Earlier in that same discussion, I attempted to let her know that whatever happened to her during her childhood was not her fault and that it is okay to be vulnerable. I acknowledged that she must have worked extremely hard as a child and that she did her best. Clearly aggravated, she dismissed or deflected everything I said and forcefully told me that there was nothing wrong with her childhood.

As I drove home that night, I had a distressing image of her as a child. I imagined that if she ever disobeyed her parents or even allowed herself to be a child, she was punished or shamed in some way. This could explain why she is guarded in talking about her relationship with her parents. And it could explain the anger and sadness I have observed in my uncles and aunt from Brunei as well. After that evening, I began to accept her more for who she is and not try to change her. I now realize that change must come from herself.

A guide for exploring your own difficult stories

You may have many stories of your own to share that you've never had the opportunity to tell. Some people walk around and pretend as though everything is fine, like I did at one time in my life. But maybe there's something in your past that's been very hurtful that people don't know about. Ask yourself why you haven't shared this. Is it fear of being judged or stigmatized? Do you feel shame? Or does it bring back too many painful feelings and memories?

I encourage you to sit down and slowly share your family stories with a professional, someone like a counsellor or family doctor who can guide you carefully through any painful experiences. I know this can be daunting, but imagine all those stored memories that are unprocessed and held inside of you like a dam holding back water. The dam will eventually crack and give way in the form of sadness, resentment, and anger towards others and yourself. Imagine if you could simply open the gates to the dam and allow everything to flow out. The built-up pressure is indeed strong and painful, but think about the relief you would feel after spending so much energy and hard work throughout your life trying to contain it. Release that pressure from yourself in a safe place and it will be your first step toward healing.

You have endured enough and maybe it's time to open up and share about your childhood. And don't worry or be afraid of what others might say or think. This is your truth and that's all that matters. No one can take those experiences away from you. No one can tell you that "it wasn't that bad," or "you made those things up," or "that's the way families were back then." It's what you experienced firsthand and those who have difficulty listening with compassion or without judgement aren't prepared or comfortable to be your support at this time.

Sit quietly by yourself, or with a trusted loved one, friend, or counsellor and look back on your childhood. Here are some sample questions to guide you in this process:

- Who hurt you (emotionally, physically, or verbally)? And how did you feel when they did?
- What was it like growing up in your household? Maybe you lived in several different homes? Again, how did you feel?
- What was the environment like for you growing up? Was it a rough and unsafe neighbourhood? Did you feel as though you belonged? There are a lot of things outside our control, especially as children.
- Who were the people you felt completely safe with? Maybe you didn't have anyone who you felt safe with. What would you have liked to receive from someone?
- Search for words to describe how you felt when people hurt you, such as: scared, frightened, sad, depressed, lonely, unsafe, humiliated, upset, confused, ashamed, or unwanted. Remember, anger is something you undoubtedly felt, but anger is a secondary emotion. It's usually started by one of the primary emotions. When we don't recognize these primary feelings they typically escalate quickly into anger.

When you share your stories, ask your listener in advance to simply listen without passing judgement or offering advice. It's time people got to know the real you and what contributed in making you the person you are today. Walls build defenses in the form of shame, but there's no shame in your childhood. Be courageous and resist letting shame consume you; refuse to allow those walls to be built. In Beverly Engel's book *It Wasn't Your Fault*, Engel identifies the most debilitating feeling in abuse as shame. Shame is deeply rooted in the secrets we hide. By sharing your stories, you will feel lighter and uplifted and you may even smile. When we expose our stories and share our truths, we no longer keep them buried inside where they build and fester in the forms of depression, anger, and anxiety. By sharing our stories, we can begin to create a normality for ourselves and begin accepting what happened to us. Soon we can process those experiences in our minds and transform them into less painful memories.

CHAPTER 2

The Awakening –
Turning The Corner

It was Wednesday, April 1st, 2015 and I was in Edmonton, Alberta for work. Another argument had taken place by phone and text between my fiancée and me. I repeatedly badgered her with angry texts throughout the night because she once again told me that I was being abusive and that I needed to stop. She pleaded with me to stop. My intense rage was fueled by each text I sent.

"Go ahead and leave! You need to get out of the apartment now!"

"You are a God damn liar and a politician!"

"You fabricate and bullshit all of your stories!"

"You've never really loved me!"

"You're a load of fuckn' bullshit!"

A day prior to my departure to Edmonton, we were in another heated argument in the apartment. I was in a blaze of fury when she didn't want to go out or do anything with me again and I complained about her lack of enthusiasm in the relationship. The argument got sidetracked by my accusations that she didn't do any of the household chores. She sat calmly on the couch listening and watching me yell in a furious rage. I snatched a bag of garbage from the kitchen and demanded that she get off the couch and take the trash out. Rightfully she refused. I immediately took the bag of garbage and tossed it onto her lap, screaming at her to take it out. She sat calmly, keeping her fear hidden, and watched the man that was once so sweet transform into a fiery and unrecognizable monster. I stormed out of the apartment in a complete rage.

Later that night, after my routine apologies and expressions of remorse, we were snuggled in bed but she wasn't comfortable making love. Once again, I instantly got enraged and accused her of not loving me. I told her she had no problem making love to other guys before me. I guilted, shamed, and blamed her for our broken relationship. An argument ensued and we went to bed without saying goodnight. I flew to Edmonton the next morning.

Despite her desperate attempts to salvage the relationship and her pleading over the phone that I get professional help, I angrily refused. Instead, I bluntly threw out blow after blow of insults, accusations, and demeaning words to her.

When I returned from my trip on Friday, she had already moved in with her parents.

I called her and asked, "So, is this it?"

She replied without hesitation, "Yep, I think so."

My heart sunk like a rock to the bottom of the ocean. I felt fear, sadness, loneliness, regret, guilt, remorse, anger, unworthiness, and self-pity. I felt complete shame for hurting the one I loved, yet I was also angry that she left. I scrolled through my texts and wished I could turn back time and take back everything I said. I missed her dearly and crumpled to the ground in tears and with the shakes.

I called her to apologize, but she would have nothing of it. I texted and wrote her a card with an admission of my faults, but still, she would have nothing of it.

I was completely heartbroken. I sent her messages reminding her of our love, desperately grasping at straws. The realization that she moved out frightened me - I was on the brink of losing my fiancée, my love, and my friend. Feelings of abandonment, worthlessness, and rejection rushed up my spine and into my heart like a powerful wave. And when the storm inside settled, memories of all the good times immediately rushed through my mind. This marked the beginning of many sleepless nights.

· · · · ·

My first questions to myself after my initial feelings were, "What's wrong with me? Why do I keep doing this?"

I began journalling my feelings like a reporter taking notes at a big social gala. I've always been fond of writing in the form of essays, query letters, and love letters. I began journalling every day for eight months straight, tracking my emotions throughout the day even while I was at work. Part of my first entry looked like this in my vulnerable state.

April 4, 2015

> "I need to forgive myself and learn to correct myself & move forward for myself. I'm so much at fault for this...I wish I could heal from this right away...I hurt my sweetheart – what's wrong with me? I feel so sorry for her."

I went on writing, "I want to heal myself and my darn childhood. I want to love myself better so I can love others and give to others without being so selfish. I need to learn to forgive myself, but what does that even look and feel like?"

Throughout my adult life I heard a lot about self-love, self-kindness, and forgiveness. I emphasize the word heard because although these words were thrown around during my relationships and were things I read on social media, I had not yet learned anything about what they mean. I'm sure you also see them either posted on someone's page, written on a sign in a gift shop, or used as part of a caption on a cat poster you've seen somewhere. It's terribly easy for any of us to simply say to our peers and kids that we need more self-love or we need to forgive ourselves. Until we know what these words mean, they are just empty words that we use to try to convince ourselves that we live by them. In later chapters we'll get into what these values have looked like for me.

Undoubtedly, I wanted my fiancée back. But there was something more. I didn't just want her back, I wanted to address something that didn't feel complete within myself. I wanted to be whole in the relationship. I wanted to change, but I wasn't sure what that looked like. I heard that abusers often claim that they promise to change and never do, but I was determined to not be another statistic. I didn't want any more empty words from myself because I knew that each time I didn't fulfill a commitment, I was losing more and more of myself down the rabbit hole. Each time I made excuses I was becoming more of a hollow man living a routine of feeling guilt, shame, and regret, and blaming others for my misfortunes. I would be fooling myself, my son, and my partners whenever I'd say, "it takes two hands to clap in a relationship" or "we were both accountable...it's always 50/50 in a relationship." But wanting to change and wanting to heal was just the beginning. The commitment to make the change in my life was the next step.

One of the most difficult things for someone who is abusive is learning to see and become cognitively aware of our own behavior. When our loved ones and partners tell us that we are treating them abusively, the words are viewed only as an attack.

In my situation, my fiancée at the time explained that calling me on the abuse was coming from a place of love. But in my mind, it was a personal attack on my credibility, behaviour, and judgement. Subconsciously, I couldn't believe that someone could give me something out of love since, throughout my childhood, my mind was programmed to think that love from my most trusted persons was either conditional or non-existent. Thus, when she explained that I was abusive, my subconscious was incapable of hearing the love that she was expressing which was, "I love you and I want to spend my life with you. And I want you to take care of yourself and heal from the abuse that you experienced – no one should have had to go through the suffering that you did. It's difficult for me to see you hurting inside so much and unless you take care of the pain that you experienced so long ago, it's no longer healthy for me to be in this relationship anymore."

Instead, what I subconsciously heard was, "you are bad, you are broken, therefore you are unlovable, and I am leaving!"

Trying to listen to my fiancée tell me how abusive I was only pushed me further away. With an increasing heart-rate, I failed to identify my primary feelings of shame, guilt, worthlessness, and embarrassment. My failure to recognize these deeper feelings meant that they quickly transformed into anger. As a result, I fought back, throwing verbal punch after punch.

Looking back, I needed to be able to identify the tensing in my body, my rushing heartrate, and my pulsating temples and bravely express my true feelings of shame, embarrassment, and guilt. Had I done that, I might have had a better chance of resolving my anger before it escalated. More importantly, had I been able to process my past properly, I might have been able to listen without feeling attacked or ashamed.

It can be extremely difficult to make a loved one aware of their abusive actions without making them feel attacked. It's a double-edged sword because telling an abusive person that their behaviour is unacceptable only reinforces their negative thought patterns that they are a bad and unlovable person. And yet the abuse they put on you should no longer be tolerated.

• • • • •

How did I come to want to change so badly? When did I come to realize all of this? The answer lies within my own *vulnerability*. In the book *Invincible* by Brian F. Martin, the author quotes Sonja Lyubomirsky, a professor of psychology in saying, "the next step after acknowledging regrets is to move on by committing ourselves to new pursuits."[4] And that is exactly what I did when I allowed myself to be vulnerable.

During my weakest emotional point, I managed to look deeply into my past and make the commitment to change. I came to the realization that I needed to do something other than make empty promises or spew out empty catch phrases like, "look yourself in the mirror" or "two steps forward, one step back." I wouldn't describe it as rock bottom because things could have gotten worse. I could have been arrested, lost my relationship with my son, lost my job, or severed my relationship with my peers and colleagues. No, it wasn't rock bottom. I'd like to emphasize this because it doesn't always mean we need to hit rock bottom to spark a change. I remember lying in bed alone on the evening of April 5ᵗʰ thinking to myself "what now?" I wasn't doing anything except staring into an empty space in my room. Ultimately, I had a few choices:

- I could continue to do nothing and lay there wallowing in my wounds and self-pity.
- I could put this all on my fiancée and continue to blame her for being overly dramatic, uncommitted, and unloving. Yes, I could certainly do that and either convince her that she was to blame or wait until she came to that realization on her own and decided to come back to me.
- I could suck it up, pack in the relationship, and move on with resentment and hate, continuing to believe that this was all her fault.
- I could explore the possibility that she was right and that I was abusive.

As you can see, some choices would have been a lot easier for me than others. I won't lie to you - the first three options occurred to me first and they were very convincing as I kept justifying my own actions by pointing out all her faults. However, after lying empty without gaining any clarity to my suffering for seemingly endless hours, I *challenged* myself. I timidly decided to google "abusive men" on my phone. I started to feel a tingle of fear as my heart beat faster. I felt a deep resistance in my head, chest, and stomach to go any further, afraid of what I might find out. Afraid. Scared. Terrified. I recognized those feelings immediately and said to myself, if I truly believe that I'm not abusive, then what am I afraid of? Clearly, I was afraid of the truth. I was afraid of what that meant for me in my relationships with my fiancée, my son, my ex-wife, my friends, my colleagues, and my family. I was afraid that everything in my 15 000 some odd days on this planet was about to be put on trial.

Holding my breath, here's what I read from one of multiple searches about abusive behaviour patterns:

> **1. Charming.** *This person quickly smothers the other with gifts and praise. He/she immediately pushes for an exclusive relationship using phrases such as "I can't live without you" or "I'll kill myself if you leave." A clear indication something is wrong.*

> **2. Jealous.** *He/she views others as a threat to the relationship and relentlessly accuses you of flirting. "I know you are having an affair." The irony is that the abuser is usually the cheater.*

> **3. Manipulative.** *Abuse and manipulation go hand-in-hand. This person easily detects vulnerability in others and uses it as a weapon to control, belittle and demean the victim. "You are weak and ugly; no wonder you were abused as a kid."*

> **4. Controlling.** *Constant checking on the whereabouts of the victim is a common trait for the abuser. "I check the mileage on your car. So don't lie to me." A male controller often*

refuses to let his girlfriend have a job, she might "meet someone."

5. A Victim. *An abuser doesn't take any responsibility for his/ her poor choices. They are never at fault. When she loses her job, or he gets into a fight, someone else is to blame. "You make me hit you" or "I drink because you stress me out."*

6. Narcissistic. *The whole world revolves around the abuser and his/her needs. This person is invigorated by the fact that the victims "walks on eggshells" and live in fear of the next outburst.*

7. Inconsistent. *Mood swings are a common trait for an abuser. One minute he/she is happy and sweet, the next they are pounding a fist or throwing a tantrum.*

8. Critical. *Verbally assaulting others is a way of life for the abuser. "You are a stupid, fat, dis-gusting tramp. You can't ever leave me; no other man would have you" or "Ha! You call yourself a man. You are nothing but a mama's boy."*

9. Disconnected. *Isolation from family and friends is a key goal for the abuser because it forces the victim into total submission. "Your family causes too much trouble for us. I don't want you seeing them anymore."*

10. Hypersensitive. *The slightest offense sends the abuser ranting. Everyone is out to "get him/her." "My boss had it in for me; I bend over backwards on my job but I still got fired."*

11. Vicious and cruel. *A significant number of abusers harm children and animals as well as a partner. Intimidation and inflicting pain fuels his/her power. "If I can't have you, no one will" or "I just pretended to love you so that you would sleep with me."*

12. Insincerely repentant. *He/she will swear to never "behave like that again." But unless an abuser receives professional help and solid accountability it's unlikely the abuse will disappear.[5]*

I went through this line by line, reluctantly but bravely recounting certain behaviours and examples of mine that matched up perfectly to each of the signs of an abuser. I didn't attempt to justify any of my behaviours with "because she did this to me" statements. I solely looked at my own actions and came to the most difficult conclusion. With wide-eyes I said out loud, "I AM abusive."

• • • • •

Most of us live in an environment where bravery and courage are determined by how strong we are in the face of danger or adversity. We are considered brave for jumping out of an airplane when we go skydiving. Women and men are regarded as brave and courageous for serving their countries in the face of war. We put on a brave face when a loved one passes on. Cancer survivors and victims are tremendously courageous for what they must endure. By no means am I minimizing the heroism required by people in any of these examples – these are, in fact, excellent examples of bravery. However, what about being vulnerable? Honestly, how many of us grew up hearing from our parents or caregivers that it is brave to be vulnerable? "Son, be brave and tell me how you're feeling?" or "Honey, be brave and cry!"

It's not very often we associate the word vulnerability with bravery. The Webster dictionary defines vulnerable as, "... capable of being physically or emotionally wounded... open to attack or damage." One of the most enduring tests to one's bravery is allowing ourselves to be "capable of feeling emotionally wounded" and being accountable for our own shortcomings. The key word is "capable."

When being vulnerable, be careful not to be self-deprecating with statements such as "I am worthless" or "I am unlovable." I am talking about being vulnerable to self-evaluate and tap into our weaknesses so we can see our behaviours and actions that have directly affected others.

We likely already know our weaknesses but need the courage to bring them to the surface and talk about them which is one the first steps in taking accountability. By being vulnerable, we no longer care about being judged because we are *capable* of feeling emotionally wounded. When we keep pressing forward and feel increasingly more vulnerable, our courage continues to grow exponentially. We are then able to self-evaluate truths and courageously begin to take accountability for our actions. We can begin to openly say things about ourselves that were previously too painful to admit. Here are some examples of difficult things you might be able to say about yourself.

- "I am abusive"
- "I am often mean to my kids and husband/wife"
- "I am controlling"
- "I have an anger problem"
- "I have a drinking problem"
- "I am depressed and I need help"
- "I am not open minded very often"
- "I am insecure and jealous"

When we are brave enough to allow ourselves to be vulnerable, our defenses are down and we are able to talk about almost anything about ourselves; we may even eventually laugh at these things. As a result, the shame is lifted and disappears because as previously mentioned, once we expose our secrets and past, shame can no longer exist. Shame is the root of why we lash out at people, why we feel we aren't good enough, and why we blame others for our misfortunes.[6]

When we have the courage to acknowledge our weaknesses, we are able to express our feelings in healthier ways. We allow ourselves to sob, laugh, be silly, and to have self-compassion – an ability I will talk about later in the book.

· · · · ·

When I lay in bed that evening in April feeling vulnerable, I found a way to let go of my shame and any judgement that came with it. It allowed me to read further about abusive behaviours and to immediately begin to research and register for workshops on anger and abuse. It allowed me to seek professional help and motivated me to want to learn more. I began to read countless books on the topic, went to counselling, and journalled every day. It certainly took a lot of courage and bravery for me to be vulnerable and I took advantage of that momentum and was able to catalyze change.

The toughest part was behind me when I was able to admit my abusive behaviours to myself. I was then able to be brave enough to share this with my fiancée, my counsellors, my son, my ex-wife, my mom, my coworkers, and my friends. I was able to hold myself accountable and, with the exception of my fiancée (for reasons that are understandable), I was not judged by a single one of them. In fact, all of them praised me for my courage and bravery.

It's not easy to come out and hold ourselves accountable for our behaviours and for being abusive. There's a fear of being stigmatized or shamed for it. There are also potential repercussions and consequences to relationships, to family pride, and maybe to our jobs. At the end of the day, it's easy for any of us to walk away from this at any time and say "I don't care anymore. I don't care about being brave and I don't care about the relationship or about getting help." The desire to walk away is understandable, and at any point in your journey you can choose to stop and go on with what you've always been doing. However, I can almost promise you that the cycle of whatever you're hurting from won't repair and end on its own. The cycle happens repeatedly by no fault of your partner, your coworkers, or your family members. How is it possible that every job you've held or every relationship you've had or every family member has been responsible for turning your life into shambles? Do you really want to continue living this way? Is it really your best and honest self? Is it your wholehearted belief that your unhappiness is someone else's fault? Or are these beliefs cultural, traditional, and antiquated?

I did not want to go through another relationship that I wasn't prepared to work for. I didn't want to have my son grow up watching me blame everyone else for my unhappiness. There is certainly a lot of stigma associated with admitting to something that's not socially popular whether it's being abusive, an alcoholic, or even depressed. However, being abusive does not summarize or define who I am. It's part of my past behaviour that I will not run away from and also just one of many things about me.

In a workshop I recently attended on mental health, I learned that one of the ways to combat stigma is to normalize it. I'm not saying that being abusive is okay. What I am saying is that getting help for being abusive and talking about it is okay and you'd be surprised by the support and encouragement you will receive regardless of what challenges you're seeking help for. When I began to normalize the truth about my abusive actions, it became easier to accept and empower myself to seek support and made it possible to change.

Connecting the dots between our childhood and our adult years

When I was in my twenties my parents thought it was a good idea to move my sister and me out while Joseph remained at home with them to be cared for because there was too much violence and anger going on. After a few months on my own (with my sister), I felt that things were great. I was working and had a fun social life with friends. I had "made it" as some would say to describe a kid who thinks he's all grown up. I was cocky, brash, and arrogant and believed that someday I would meet a nice girl, get married, have kids, and continue to be happy. Life was great because I was no longer in a household filled with abuse and shame. I also didn't want to speak to my parents anymore and I was literally separated from my problems. I actually thought my belief system was becoming my own and was a healthy one.

The only issue with that philosophy was that I was only *physically* separated from my problems. What I went through as a child and in my teenage years affected me more deeply than what I was able to see. My challenges and issues growing up were buried in my subconscious and followed me everywhere I went regardless of whether or not I was living with my parents. My internalized rage, anger, and shame would only come to the surface in my intimate relationships.

It can be difficult to recognize when you are going through an internal struggle with your beliefs. After all, you might be on a road in your life that you're generally very content with. Your parents raised you the best they could and provided you with what they thought was a healthy, or at least acceptable, environment. They raised you with principles, values, and beliefs based on what they were taught when they were children. We picked up on these lessons, live by them today, and transfer them to our partners and kids. We subconsciously model our caregivers' beliefs and values because that's what we were taught and exposed to during our childhood. If we have an unhealthy belief system it's extremely difficult to change because subconsciously we are fixed on believing it is healthy.

Again, you might say, "I'm fine with my life. My partner and I argue from time to time and for the most part I'm fine with the people at work. I sometimes have to yell at them to get the job done, but that's what being a leader is about. My kids are fine. Yeah, I sometimes get angry and lecture them and sometimes get really impatient with my partner. Who doesn't? There are some things I can't stand but it's normal. It's all part of life and being a parent and wife/husband!"

And perhaps that's all working well for you and your family. After all, we all have such different lives and upbringings with different standards, values, and beliefs. Sometimes not knowing or not being aware is a blessing. But challenge yourself, take a step back and bravely evaluate your situation; ask yourself if these behaviours are becoming a pattern and the norm rather than the exception.

In the 1999 movie the Matrix, the hero, Neo, has to make a decision whether to continue living the life he knows or take a coloured pill which will help him see the truth about life in the Matrix. The prospect of seeing this truth is frightening and uncertain, yet liberating. In real life, we don't have magic coloured pills to help us see the truth, but we do have our courage and bravery to help us see a clearer picture. This next simple exercise can help you along the way.

I will ask you to draw some parallels between your behaviours and beliefs growing up with what you might be experiencing today.

Here are three examples of how my past beliefs are linked to my present ones.

Example 1

Childhood years: When I was growing up, it was frowned on to listen to pop music at a high volume. The associated beliefs my parents taught me was that pop music was for unruly kids and listening to it meant being rebellious and disobedient. If we were caught listening to loud pop music, there were fearful consequences.

Adult years: When I listen to music in the car or at home, it's typically on the softer side. When my fiancée played loud music, I felt bothered and uncomfortable. In my subconscious, my beliefs from when I was young made me believe that it's unruly and disobedient to play loud music because it is not acceptable behaviour.

Example 2

Childhood years: I grew up in a household with a lot of arguments, shouting, yelling, and shoving. Slamming doors and pounding on walls to get attention was something that occurred often. The attached beliefs were dominance and strength.

Adult years: Phone conversations with my mom and dad are often irate, filled with shouting, blame, and anger. I also sometimes argued with my sister when we lived together at the apartment. The violent behaviours were associated with my subconscious beliefs of dominance, strength, and being right.

Example 3

Childhood years: My parents, particularly my dad, were extremely strict. Whenever I was playing, laughing, and being silly, I was often discouraged with verbal warnings, yelling, and frowning scowls that made me hold my breath in fear. My parents did not participate in Halloween. They refused to give out candy to kids, thus the house was always the darkest one on the block without a single light turned on. My mom and dad would get angry when kids rang the doorbell and would say things like, "they should know better not to come!"

My older brother and sister echoed their beliefs. Hence, we were not allowed to go out trick-or-treating although in my heart I always wanted to. I was too afraid to ask fearing I would be disobeying their beliefs. The only thing I could do on Halloween was to go downstairs in the dark basement and peek outside through a crack in the curtains no more than a few inches wide to make sure no one would see me. I would stand there by the window observing the wonderfully decorated costumes, the happy families, and the kids screaming and laughing as they passed our house. Even when it wasn't Halloween, on the other 364 days of the year, my parents repeatedly told us not to stand and look outside the living room window, fearing people would see what we were doing. I never quite understood what was behind this message but obeyed them nonetheless. There must have been some paranoia my parents had about being viewed by the public that I never understood and still don't, even to this day.

Adult years: I have often viewed people as threats. I rarely give people the benefit of the doubt at first and I find myself quietly analyzing them from every possible angle before opening up to them. I can be shy and afraid of being judged or laughed at. I sometimes question the motives of anyone who wants to get to know me. This sense of not being worthy or likeable has at times plagued my adult social life, making it difficult for me to openly trust people, thinking that they could be malicious. I tend to be on guard just in case my judgement of them is correct and they decide to lash out, insult, or shame me. Thus, the irony is that I'm making assumptions about who they could be instead of welcoming them as new people into my life. In social situations with people I've never met before, I can be a wall flower. Those that aren't interested in talking to me must therefore be "bad" people. As a result, my self-talk would tell me that I'm not likeable and not worthy. My anger would quickly follow and I would begin criticizing those people with harsh and judging words.

Thus, the parallels between my childhood beliefs and adult behaviours are clear and undeniably true. As a child, I was subconsciously programmed to be fearful of people. I was taught that being a kid, acting silly, and celebrating with others should be approached with extreme caution or there would be consequences.

Speaking of celebrations, Christmases and birthdays are some other deeply rooted challenges of mine that I recently discovered. Growing up, Christmases and birthdays were not particularly joyful experiences or memories. My mom would almost always work on Christmas day for the triple time pay despite my pleas to have her home on Christmas. We weren't allowed to open presents until my mom was home from work, usually around 4 or 5 p.m. And this was providing we were "good" and "well-behaved." Typically, I would get a total of about four or five wrapped presents from my parents, aunts, and family friends. After opening the presents, we weren't allowed to open and play with all the toys. My mom would usually allow us only one toy that we could open and play with while the rest were to be stored or given away. This always disappointed and frustrated me because I always thought that the gifts were for me. My mom would come up with reasons such as, "you're too old for that toy" or "you'll only play with it once and never touch it again."

I was often lectured and shamed for even asking for the present I wanted for Christmas whether it was an electronic hockey game or Lego. Thus, each Christmas, I had a lot of disappointment knowing that I would only be allowed to enjoy one or two of my presents. And when we were older, Christmas was especially difficult when my brother was deeply affected by his mental health problems. During the early years of his mental illness, I was fearful of going downstairs. I would wait until I knew it was safe and the fighting, incoherent yelling, and arguments had stopped. Thus, during those Christmases opening gifts was a very private affair of quickly going downstairs, opening my gifts, and going back upstairs into my room.

My memories of my childhood birthdays are also painful. Again, my mom would almost always work on my birthday. I honestly do not remember much about these days in terms of them being celebrations. I don't recall getting gifts from my parents other than a gift card to the Hudson Bay restaurant where my mom worked which included a free birthday ice cream with the face of a clown decorated on it. My sister gave me gifts and her kindness is perhaps my only fond birthday memory. My mom would cook a big dinner, get a cake, and ask my aunts and uncles to come over, but there was never a point made that it was for my birthday. I remember many tearful birthday mornings having not received any presents from my parents. I never felt that my birthday was a day to celebrate or enjoy.

One birthday I wanted to go to Chuck E. Cheese's and my dad did not approve. He was against us going to the arcade and thought those places are for unruly and rowdy kids. I'm not sure if it was sympathy or a message from my mom, but he eventually caved in. He pulled out his wallet, handed my Uncle Stephen some cash, and asked him to take me there. I felt guilty and ashamed because I knew my dad didn't approve and I felt as though it was my fault for compromising his belief system and inconveniencing him.

Finally, there were some birthdays when I remember getting a beating from my dad.

As an adult, I have found myself pushing March 11th away as though it's a day that's not worth celebrating. I usually make the excuse that I don't like being in the spotlight. I remember one year when I was at my friend Sandra's house and a bunch of us were chatting about birthdays. It happened to be my birthday that day and when I told them they were not only surprised but confused why I didn't want to make a big deal of it.

More painfully, one year my ex-wife, Pearl, had organized a wonderful birthday lunch celebration at the Boathouse with some coworkers of mine. It was supposed to be a surprise but I somehow found out about it. I kept making excuses that I needed to get a haircut and couldn't make the lunch. She went out of her way to reschedule the time with my friends and an argument between us ensued. I eventually made it to the luncheon, though reluctantly, but not without creating some painful scars.

Days before my 43rd birthday, my fiancée at the time and I got into another big argument which turned out to be one of the last ones before our official breakup. Of all things, we argued over the type of birthday cake I wanted. She wanted to lovingly bake me a cake of my choice. One of my favourites is black forest cake, but she asked that I select a more traditional birthday cake for her to make. I couldn't subconsciously accept her love and we argued over the cake until I eventually got furious and told her to not bake me anything at all. Instead, I went to the supermarket and bought my own black forest cake for my birthday. I'm quite sure that subconsciously I wanted the argument to happen to push her away. My sense of self-worth was low and I didn't feel that I was worth celebrating. Immediately after the argument she told me, "You do this every single birthday! You need to do something about that!"

Naturally in my closed-minded state, I ignored her comment at the time. Months later, however, I realized that she couldn't have been more correct. My subconscious was telling me that I'm unworthy of a birthday celebration, of being celebrated for any reason, or of being loved. I felt I needed to earn my birthday and earn my worthiness to be happy and celebrated. I subconsciously believed that celebrating my birthday was conditional on me being on my best behaviour and that I needed to make sure I don't inconvenience anyone just for me.

The parallels are uncanny and undeniably true. We are today who we were taught to become, warts and all. Have a look at examples of times when you have caused others a lot of strife and grief and you will be amazed by how they might be connected to experiences you had as a child. Once you have identified a few of these experiences in your life, you can begin connecting the dots between past and present and can empower yourself by taking control and being accountable for some of the unhappiness and displeasures in your life. You can acknowledge that the past events of abuse were never your fault. You no longer need to behave according to those false beliefs that you are worthless and unlovable.

CHAPTER 3

Fire Breathing With Abuse And Shaming – My Adult Years

Approximately 1 in 100 people develop schizophrenia, usually in their late teens to early twenties.[7] Schizophrenia is a debilitating disease that affects the brain. Over time, it takes away the brain's function to conduct what we see as normal, everyday behaviour. Some symptoms include delusions (false beliefs), hallucinations (hearing voices or seeing images that don't actually exist), mood swings, and disorganized thoughts that can lead to disruptive behaviour and prevent the person from having clear, coherent communication. Although it's not clearly known what the cause is, it is believed that genetics plays a big part in it.

There are three phases to the disease: prodromal, active, and residual. In the prodromal stage, people with schizophrenia may lose interest in their daily activities. They may become reclusive from friends and family members. Concentrating can be difficult because they are often confused. In the active phase, hallucinations may occur. Distorted thoughts can lead to unusual behaviour and can be frightening to the person with the disease and to others. Finally, the residual phase is similar to the prodromal phase except amplified and even more difficult to manage.

There is a heavy stigma surrounding this unfortunate disease. People with schizophrenia are falsely portrayed by the media as psychotic killers and rapists. Ironically, patients with schizophrenia are unlikely to cause harm to anyone other than themselves.

My brother - the later years

My brother started to develop obvious symptoms of schizophrenia in his early twenties. He came back from university one summer and he was noticeably different. He had a part time job at the bank and had a difficult time staying focused; he was sometimes sent home due to miscalculating funds. My dad would immediately get angry and impatient. He would scold and shame him in front of all of us. My sister and I would get into arguments with Joseph and call him hurtful names like "stupid" and "crazy" to name a few. His behaviour was complex, unpredictable, and confusing. In my early teen years, I didn't know that his behaviour was any different than when he was just being a jerk of a brother again. We often argued and fought with irate shouting matches.

One day he came into my room while I was playing on the computer and said, "Guess what? I just saw an apparition!" Frightened, I ignored him and spent less and less time talking to him. He would constantly go in and out of the house. He would leave, lock the door, and within minutes, come back. Then he'd go out again and come back, over and over again.

In my late teens when my mom and dad had already gone to work and Jackie had left for school, I was left alone with him in the mornings. Early in the morning I would listen to him shout and have irrational, angry discussions with his TV programs. He would shout, "STOP chastising me! I know who you are!" Even more frightened, I would stay hidden in my room until it was time to head out to school. For years I felt suffocated, frightened, and confined in my own space at home trying to filter out his presence and disruptive behaviour. When he entered the same room as me, I would stop what I was doing and go to another room in the house as far away as possible so I couldn't hear his random and angry outbursts.

I would finally feel free at home when Joseph went out. I would be myself again and allowed myself out of the bedroom with a feeling of immense relief. But the moment he came home, I would quickly disappear back to my room feeling frightened unless a fight ensued between him and another member of the family. By the time I went to university, the daily routine included me yelling at him for being "stupid", shaming him for not being able to get things right, and wishing he was gone from our lives. Jackie was equally cruel. Round and round it went like this, every day for years. My dad and mom would get into arguments with him. My *Ah-cow* visiting from Toronto would yell and shout at him, calling him lazy and useless. By this time, I was allowed to have friends over to watch movies; even they would make fun of him, calling him "Psycho Joe." The pain and cruelty that I inflicted on him fills me with immense guilt and regret.

One fateful night, another argument got out of hand. He started shoving Jackie and I ran downstairs to try to break up the fight. He wouldn't stop, even when dad and mom intervened. I desperately ran upstairs to my parents' bedroom and nervously dialed 911. I remember speaking to the operator pleading for help and for someone to come over right away. After I got off the phone dad ran upstairs, grabbed me, and reamed me out, shouting, "WHY did you do that?!" I couldn't take any more of it and if my parents weren't able to do anything about it, I knew I had to.

My brother spent the night in custody which triggered the start of him getting the long overdue help he needed. He was in and out of the hospital for years and during this time, resentment increasingly grew within me. I resented my parents for not doing anything about it earlier and for not seeking help. Instead they would be off to their ballroom dance lessons while I would be hiding in the bedroom. I resented my brother for hurting us and for all the fights. My own fear, hurt, and ignorance made it impossible for me to accept him. My parents were in constant denial and would tell me, "Don't tell anyone about Joseph! Just tell them that he went out" whenever house guests came over. My father insisted that my brother was mentally well and a few times tried to explain his decline in mental health by saying that people at university gave him drugs.

This denial weighed heavily on me in the form of shame. Even years later I sometimes denied that I had a brother. My brother was apprehended one time at the Montreal airport when he decided to take one of his several questionable trips. When my parents moved my sister and me out so they could look after my brother, my resentment was at its peak. I blamed my parents at the time for loving him more than us. Ironically, I was comfortable living at home at the time with my parents; but as it turns out, it was probably best that I didn't.

I didn't tell anyone about my brother's schizophrenia until I was around 41 when I told my fiancée at the time. Even then, the information was somewhat spotty as I was filled with shame and fear of judgement. I realize now that there is no shame in talking about it. It's a tragic disease that has sadly taken away my brother. He didn't receive the compassion or love he needed from me or my family.

I've now broken out of that shell and I talk openly about Joseph with friends, coworkers, my ex-wife, and my son. I have even read up on the disease and actively participated in a mental health workshop to help reduce stigma. For the most part, everyone has been tremendously compassionate to him, me, and the family.

To this day, I struggle to reach out to my brother. He calls my mom every day, but I am still plagued with hurt, fear, and guilt for what's transpired in the past. In a household marred by abuse, there wasn't a whole lot of space for healing and love. I hope to someday be able to say I'm sorry to him, although it will never make up for what he has suffered. I only have love, sorrow, and compassion for him now and it hurts deeply to think about him and what he lost. I finally, after all these years, accept that I have a brother who has schizophrenia. His illness is a tragedy but I will no longer be ashamed of him. This is a journey that I know I will continue to work on which will require a different form of bravery on my part. It's a slow process, but I believe I'm one step closer to connecting with him again.

It's important for me to point out that healing is something that takes time and does not happen overnight. We see weight loss pills or money-making schemes that have immediate results. Healing your past, your relationship with yourself and your relationship with others takes time, effort, and strength. Be patient with yourself and try not to get overwhelmed by what you still struggle with. Focus on the present moment and the healing you have already experienced by talking, sharing, and objectively observing your life.

My relationships

In my mid-twenties I met a wonderful girl named Pearl. She was smart, beautiful, and sexy, and I immediately knew there was something between us when I caught her smiling in my direction. We met at a Chinese dinner and dance banquet that her family had organized, and we hit it off right away. Three years later we got married and had as part of our wedding a big traditional Chinese dinner with 600 guests. Yes, 600 (I think only 20 guests were friends of mine and hers) - I believe Prince William and Kate Middleton's wedding had fewer guests.

Pearl was the first true relationship I had. After a beautiful courtship and honeymoon phase, still months before the wedding, something started to change. I was getting increasingly short-tempered and irritated with her, arguing with her and blaming her for being tardy or not remembering what I specifically told her.

After we were married, I often used imperatives like "should" and "you have to." We argued constantly when we moved in together and when she was pregnant with our son, Josh, causing her additional strain. I was never satisfied with how the apartment was kept and complained about junk in the home and how meals needed to be prepared. I raged on and on until one night, when Josh was about 7 months old, he was crying at night and I demanded that she look after him. She did so and replied, "let me know when you want to sign the divorce papers!" and stormed away to another room with our son in her arms.

We were married for just over a year when she left. I was devastated and torn apart at the loss, and my heart ached even more because she took our son with her. For a number of years, I unknowingly lived alone in depression and with little desire for social interaction. I refused to talk about it with my best friends, Vincent and Sandra, or with coworkers. I didn't talk to a professional and decided what was best for me was to keep my problems to myself. This was how I had always tried to manage my emotional problems.

Fortunately, I was able to see my son but he was still quite young and I needed to bring him home to Pearl every time I saw him. I would do my best to play an active role in his life and to look after him, raise him, play with him, help him take naps and take him to playgrounds and playdates. I eventually taught him how to ride a bike and I even promised him I'd do so in seven short lessons. He smirked at me and said, "My friend Max said his dad could teach him to ride in six days!" and we both laughed.

He was the one person in my life who I took great pride in. However, I had many downfalls in my parenting skills. I spanked him less than a handful of times, but that was a handful of times too many. Whenever he spilt a drink, forgot to put away a game or toy or didn't come when I asked him to, I found myself passively sighing, fussing, or snapping at him and saying, "Josh! You SHOULD know better!" or, "You're a big boy now!" I was short tempered and easily irritated by the slightest thing he did that didn't please me.

On the other hand, I often expressed my love for him both verbally and through physical signs of affection. I wanted to give him everything I didn't receive from my parents. He was showered with toys for his birthdays and Christmases and I made sure I spent quality time playing with him and educating him. What I didn't realize was how abusive I was subconsciously capable of being. Like a Dr. Jekyll and Mr. Hyde syndrome, it was painful and confusing for him to navigate who he was getting as a dad.

One summer day we spent a fun-filled day at the beach with some friends. Josh, aged 7, mistakenly lost his flip flops in the sand and we looked everywhere and couldn't find them. I got so angry with him I began yelling at him as we were leaving and immediately grabbed him and carried him to the car. In the car, I went berserk and raged on him shamefully. I ripped into him about being irresponsible and about not taking care of his own belongings and I yelled at him for losing his flip-flops. I then proceeded to yell at him for not being responsible enough to put away his toys and his guitar at home. He wept and cried with fear and shame. He cried and cried like I never heard before and all I could do was ream him out even more, louder and louder. He pleaded with me to call his mom and he tearfully begged her to come pick him up. He pleaded helplessly buckled in his car seat. I shudder with fear and disappointment in myself when I think back to that day and my false sense of power, my superiority, and my abusiveness. There was nothing acceptable about my behaviour that day.

On another occasion, we went for a hike with my cousin visiting from Toronto. We wanted to hike up the Chief, which is a 45 minute drive north of Vancouver. My son was around 9 years old at the time. By the time we reached the first 100 or 200 metres of the hike, he started to gasp for air. He gasped and requested water to pour on his head. I got angry and snapped at him, "DON'T waste that water! What do you mean you can't hike this? You should be able to!"

Because he couldn't continue on the hike, we headed back down the mountain and drove back home. I reamed him out again in the car for his failure and if it wasn't for my cousin being there, things could have been much worse.

I would show and verbalize my frustration and disappointment when he spilled juice on the countertop or if he was walking a little slow and couldn't keep up. When he took tae kwon do at aged 7, I showed disappointment in my face when he didn't do well during a class or a test. All of this left a lasting scar of sadness and anxiety in him that I am accountable for. That's what verbal and emotional abuse does. It strips away dignity and self-esteem and it is as damaging as, or more than, physical abuse.

Shortly after my relationship ended with Pearl, I recognized I had an anger problem. I read a book or two and stopped with that, believing I had taken care of everything inside of me. Because I didn't look deep enough within myself, my management of my anger and my lack of understanding would haunt me again in a later relationship.

In 2013, I met a wonderful and gorgeous woman. She was a teacher and was intelligent, funny, sweet, sexy, and determined. She simply made my eyes light up at the very sight of her. Our relationship was incredibly passionate and loving at the start, and within eight months we were engaged. It was a beautiful time in our relationship and we had a lot of fun exploring our city, and going on road trips. She was the one person who opened up my world to counselling and to talking about my childhood and my brother's illness. She provided me with a safe and compassionate space for beginning to address the challenges

I faced growing up. She was certainly the catalyst in my healing. She made it easier for me to talk about my past suffering because she also grew up in an abusive household and dealt with her own childhood challenges. Like most relationships in the early stages, our love flourished and we were head over heels for each other. We assumed we were well on our way to a bright future together.

However, as the relationship progressed my abusive behaviour started to take over, often fueled by insecurities and control. Feeling that I needed someone to love me and to constantly remind me of this love was one of my many weaknesses. Feeling insecure, needing attention at parties and analyzing every detail of the things people said about me made it impossible for the relationship to have any sense of longevity. I made her feel guilty and shamed her for having friends who I didn't like. I shamefully and outrageously criticized her choices of past boyfriends, claiming that she loved them more than me. I even attempted to control how much alcohol she drank. I blamed her for my unhappiness and for not being adventurous enough with me, even demanding sex a few times followed by guilt if she didn't comply. I took my anger out and was often short tempered with her for things that had nothing to do with her. I would come home from work and be irritated and angry over the smallest things such as laundry that was lying around or dirty dishes. I would find reasons to be angry with her, rejecting almost everything including the biggest smiles and kisses anyone has ever given me. Not only was it a shameful time for me, but more importantly, a debilitating and humiliating time for her. I simply robbed her of her dignity.

An Evening of rage

I was hell frightening sometimes. One fine evening my fiancée and I were getting ready to go to a fundraiser at a local pub. It was a casual event but nonetheless we still did our best to dress up for the occasion which for me meant a nice hot shower, fresh boxers, and a bit of mouthwash to freshen up my aging breath. Typically, just before social engagements with strangers or people I wasn't comfortable with, I had a tendency to do one or a combination of the following:

- think about how bored, disinterested, and nervous I was going to feel during the event;
- find reasons not to go or create legit reasons to cop out;
- shut down and not want to talk or do much throughout the day;
- get irritable and start an argument unrelated to the event;
- pout and show resentment through my facial expressions; and
- blame everyone for my unhappiness.

Because the event was a fundraiser that was put together by the school where she worked, I wasn't going to know anyone there other than her. This meant that I would cling to her like a new found puppy, minus the cuteness factor.

As I was showering, we started talking about the evening. My mind began racing in all directions, aimlessly, like a chicken with its head cut off. My ridiculous thoughts ran wild fraught by my insecurities and fears that my fiancée would run off with someone at the pub who was a million times more dashing and charismatic than I was. An argument ensued, and out of frustration, she finally turned around and sarcastically replied, "MAYBE I WILL!"

Like a fired-up beast ready to pounce, I ripped down the shower curtain and roared, *"GET THE HELL OUT OF HERE!"*

Horrified, she disengaged and went to the other room. I jumped out of the shower and followed her while I was dripping wet. I continued on my rampage, badgering her about how she doesn't love me and this is not what love is (which is ironic given that I was naked, wet, and yelling at her about what love is).

Like a person who had just sprinted a hundred metres, I eventually ran out of breath. We miraculously patched things up an hour or so later and eventually made it to the fundraiser unscathed for the rest of the evening. But like all major arguments, it left a lasting scar that was irreparable.

• • • • •

When I could finally acknowledge and accept that I had been abusive, it sparked a change in my inner awareness and motivated me to seek professional help. However, taking action to change myself while maintaining a relationship with someone who I had hurt was a difficult balancing act.

After my fiancée moved out after almost two years of living together, the relationship continued to sputter on for another year plagued with arguments and times when one of us would storm out of a restaurant, creating a public scene.

However difficult, I knew I still needed to move forward with my own healing and continue to acknowledge my mistakes. During the countless hours, days, and months of individual therapy, I identified and acknowledged how cruel and harmful my behaviours were. One of the things I needed to do was to hold myself accountable for my abuse. This included openly sharing and apologizing to her for being abusive, and citing specific examples with no excuses or justification. I even held myself accountable and spoke to her father who was so sickened by my admission that he asked me to get out of his house immediately. I also openly shared and apologized to my friends, my son, and even my ex-wife for the abuse I had put them through over the years and made sure they knew they did nothing wrong and did not deserve the treatment they received from me.

Anger and abuse

As I have already mentioned, anger is a secondary emotion. It's a myth that we go from a state of calm to one of anger immediately. There's actually a fraction of a second between calm and anger where there's a primary feeling that we fail to recognize. There are various levels of anger (imagine a scale of 1 to 10) and it's an emotion that can be useful in the event of true danger. Anger comes from the most primitive part of our brain: the "fight or flight" part (amygdala). But if suppressed anger from our painful experiences as children is not properly processed, it can become incredibly damaging during our adult years.

Not only does anger humiliate you and make you feel guilty afterwards, it more importantly creates indelible negative memories for the other person. I'm sure to this day my son has terrifying memories of going to the beach and going on that hike with me. I've spoken to him and apologized for these incidents many times since then, and especially in the past year when I have held myself accountable for being abusive, but it does not take away these negative experiences.

Similarly, my fiancée and I went away one Christmas to a place in Washington State called Quinault Lodge. It was a beautiful and romantic spot and a lovely gift from her. On the way there we got into a heated argument and I raged on about her past and on the topic of gifts. The argument got off track and took a life of its own. We continued arguing back and forth all the way there until we checked into the room that night. I got so terrifyingly irate and verbally abusive, she almost decided to sleep on the sofa in the lobby that night, fearing for her safety. Although we eventually reconciled because of her selfless attempt to make the best of a situation, the memory of that place is haunted by my horrific and abusive behaviour. She was robbed of any positive experiences or memories from this getaway.

Repeated patterns of anger can lead to abuse. Recognizing abusive behaviour is painful. It's painful because it brings up feeling of unworthiness, self-hate, and self-anger which is why it's so difficult to come to terms with it. Abuse can take on many forms. It can be physical, emotional, verbal, or sexual abuse. Abusive behaviour typically follows a pattern, called the abuse cycle, as outlined here.

1. **Tension** – For unexplained reasons, tension at home can build up. You become irritable and quick to lash out over trivial things such as laundry, dirty dishes, or noise in the house. The tension builds up and the victim often feels like he/she is "walking on eggshells" and must be careful of what he/she says and does. There's an aura of fear and unpredictability created. Good news can easily be drowned out by this tension. Stress builds up and soon the entire household recognizes that they need to tread lightly around you.

2. **Violence** – This is the stage when you pop. You rage, yell, shout, snap, insult, punch, slap, beat, put-down, or show others "who's boss."

3. **Honeymoon** – After your storm has passed and the victims concede to the abuse, you feel guilty inside. You feel ashamed of how hurt you made the other person feel and you apologize. You treat the victims kindly, gently, and even laugh with them to lighten the mood. You might even minimize the violence or deny it to convince the victim that nothing is wrong. This is the stage when the abuser promises change, but the promises don't last.

4. **Normalcy** – During this stage, life resumes to its ordinary state. Dishes are done without complaint, the kids are fed, and laughter once again resumes. However, due to unprocessed thoughts and lack of proper treatment, this stage of

normalcy won't last. Eventually, tension will build up again and restart the abuse cycle.

Abuse can take many forms. Just because someone does not physically assault someone else does not mean they're not abusive. Verbal abuse with name-calling intended to put-down the other person is a form of abuse. Shaming and calling the person a "loser" or an "idiot" are examples of verbal abuse. Emotional abuse can be in the form of control which I talk about in later chapters. It's a psychological form of abuse where the person can be made to feel worthless or unattractive by your controlling words.

Those of us who are perpetrators of abuse must recognize that as much as our behaviours are wrong in terms of hurting the victims, we owe it to ourselves to seek help. If we continue to be in denial of our abusive behaviours, we also deny ourselves our true potential. There is so much love, worth, and goodness we can discover once we begin to recognize and take accountability for our actions. I share tips in later chapters on where to get started.

Perpetrators of abuse are strongly advised to attend individual or group therapy. Couple's counselling is not recommended because it enables the abuser's behaviours by sharing accountability with the victim. In other words, couple's counselling tells the victim that it's their fault too and justifies some of the actions of the abuser. Abusive behaviour needs to be managed separately. It is also recommended that victims seek support independently.

• • • • •

I have a friend who shared a story with me about her husband who came home from work one day and was non-communicative. She asked him if he was ready to go to her mom's house for dinner and he replied with a stern, "No."

She continued to sheepishly ask him if he was going to go.

He callously replied again, saying, "No."

Disappointed, frightened and hurt, she decided to head out to her mom's house on her own. Moments after she got into the car, her husband unexpectedly came outside and got into the car without saying a single word. She continued to think that it might have been something she said or did.

The next day, her husband apologized and said that he had had a bad day at work. His anger resulted in him being rude to his wife because he couldn't overcome the pain and articulate what his primary feelings were which were likely frustration, resentment, and maybe embarrassment. Had he identified those feelings, he likely would have been able to kindly express to his wife, "I feel frustrated and upset from work today. It's got nothing to do with you, but I don't feel like talking about it. I'm not really in the mood to go to your mom's but I'll do my best to go."

I want to point out that when we feel anger, we need to ask ourselves what the primary emotion underlying this anger is. You'd be surprised that by simply identifying the primary feeling, you have the opportunity to soothe the anger and prevent it from escalating and exploding.

Anger is often followed by guilt, followed by redemption and overwhelming kindness. By identifying your primary feelings and linking them to events or situations in your past, you can understand yourself better and the source of where the anger and abuse is coming from. If you had childhood experiences where anger was the emotion used to resolve conflict, there's a likelihood that you will default to that as well. With that awareness, you will find that your mind will slow down from that feeling of anger and self-soothe and say to yourself, "I don't need to get angry at something that isn't threatening to me. Anger isn't my real voice talking...this is likely a reaction that I experienced from my past. My true self is not like this."

There have been so many consequences of anger and abusiveness that have plagued my life. Because of my inability to manage my anger, I have been verbally abusive to colleagues at work, I have shamed and inappropriately raged against my son, and my relationships with my wife and later my fiancée failed. I have hurt my family members and I am emotionally distant from all of them. I have even hurt my friends with my angry outbursts. This may sound familiar to you as well. Just as importantly, anger has made me suffer in silence as I have sat alone feeling guilty after each angry outburst.

Anger exercise

The next time you feel angry, stop and take a moment and ask yourself: "What am I really feeling besides anger?"

Example: I'm stuck in traffic, running late to take my son to a doctor's appointment. I feel angry, but when I stop to assess my underlying primary feelings, I identify much more. What I was really feeling was anxiety and worry that I might be late for the appointment. I was also feeling frustrated by the traffic jam. Recognizing those primary feelings helps to put my mind at ease and in control. But if I don't slow down and identify those primary feelings, adrenaline and anger can quickly take over and I will begin to externalize my feelings instead of taking responsibility for them. I could become angry at the driver in front of me, angry for the appointment being so far out of the city, and angry that I couldn't get out of work earlier. I could even get angry at my son for having an ailment.

· · · · ·

What I didn't know was that my angry outbursts and how I manage my relationships are closely linked to things I faced growing up. They are related to how I was spoken to and punished by my abusers and bullies. As a child, I was an innocent victim of all the consequences of the abuse and shame. As an adult, I am accountable for my actions and therefore I must process those circumstances. If not, I will perpetually find displeasure with everything and everyone and not be able to move forward in life. In later chapters I further discuss the need to accept our past.

As a survivor of childhood abuse, I subconsciously saw myself as worthless and unlovable and I needed to be on the defensive from people who got emotionally close to me. In a perfect world, our caregivers are the most trusted and safest people we have. For the most part, they have good intentions in raising us to the best of their abilities. However, if we were not provided with healthy beliefs about ourselves, our adult minds will default to a defensive mode when triggered by fear, danger, or stress. Being on the defensive can mean unpredictable fits of anger, rage, anxiety, and depression.

The abuse I experienced as a child ran deep inside of me and subconsciously affected me as an adult in two main ways. Firstly, I struggled with criticism and jokes at my expense. Whether I was innocently told that "I'm a sensitive guy" or teased as the punchline of a harmless joke, I got very defensive and snapped back with a sharp and sarcastic tongue that made sure the other person received twice as much hurt as I had. In other words, I couldn't laugh at myself because a joke at my expense simply reminded me of the bullying and taunts I faced.

For my 26th birthday, a buddy of mine somehow managed to get a picture of me from grade 8 and, as a joke, printed it onto my birthday cake. Needless to say, I took offense to it, didn't respond well, and attempted to deflect and mock him instead. With a fiery rage burning inside of me, I couldn't accept that my grade 8 picture shows a geeky and scrawny kid with thick glasses and a god-awful haircut (who isn't embarrassed by their grade 8 picture, right?).

Secondly and perhaps more damagingly, I could not accept compliments as an adult. As ludicrous as it sounds, whenever someone complimented me by saying, "nice shirt," "I like your new glasses," or even, "happy birthday," I would shut down and not pay a word of gratitude. Inside my head, I was cautious and careful of accepting other people's kindness. I subconsciously believed there would be a catch to their generosity and at times it stirred up negative experiences I faced as a child. In fact, I remember times as an adult when I even seriously told people to "shut up!" after they complimented me on a nice haircut because I falsely believed they were being sarcastic. Getting a haircut as a kid often generated a painful experience for me. I was teased by my brother and the kids at school for having a bowl-cut for my hair, and the feelings of humiliation lingered into my adult years.

Because I did not process my past in a healthy way, as an adult I defaulted to feelings of fear, danger, or distress when dealing with conflict and people. I didn't see others as having my best interests in mind and I couldn't entirely trust them which led to my destructive behaviours.

Books, workshops, and counselling sessions on relationships and anger all say the same thing about our past: it needs to be properly processed. Our brains need to put traumatic experiences into a processed state so we are no longer stuck in those unhealed and painful memories. When I was abused by my caregivers and humiliated by bullies as a child, I didn't realize how angry I was at them. As an adult, I subconsciously relive those painful moments by projecting those experiences onto others. In doing so, all my suppressed feelings are released in the form anger, rage, and hurt. The subconscious intent is to right that which has been wronged. This of course, can never happen by subjecting others to abuse and objectively you can see how flawed the logic is. Again, this thought process is taking place in our subconscious. Thus, this emphasizes the importance of processing the hurt and the suppressed emotions from our past.

Example #1

Imagine some of the painful feelings such as fear, shame, and guilt that I faced as a child. As an adult, my mind was conditioned to go into anger mode whenever I had feelings that related to the hurtful and unprocessed experiences from my past. For example, when my fiancée innocently laughed at me for spilling juice on the kitchen floor, I immediately felt humiliated. Humiliation is a feeling I experienced a lot as a child when bullied. Because the experience was not properly processed, that humiliation translated into anger and resulted in an argument with my partner even though she never intended to hurt me.

Example #2

When I was a child my family sometimes used to drive across the border to Bellingham, Washington to go shopping. Whenever we reached the border crossing, my parents would yell, *"mo-cho"* and *"mo-gung-yeh"* because the border guards would get extremely angry and irate. I remember dad would be frantic about getting our receipts in order from purchases we made. He'd pull over at a rest station a few miles before the crossing, scramble to organize our purchases in the trunk so that they were in order, and yell at my mom and us kids, "Where's the receipt for that appliance we bought?!" or "Don't put that there! Put it THERE instead!" When we reached the border guard, my heart would race and I would hold my breath and stay completely still and silent. It used to frighten me to look in the general direction of the border guard. Sometimes I closed my eyes and pretended I was asleep to avoid the entire experience.

Prior to me processing these experiences, I used to feel tense, nervous, and anxious when I crossed the border into Bellingham as an adult. I'd fear having any conversations in the car with anyone who was travelling with me and I'd turn the radio completely off and sit still. However, after properly processing those memories, I'm able to focus on my breath and identify with the anxious sensations running through my body to remind myself that my reaction is merely a trigger from my past. Within minutes the sensations usually subside and the experience becomes less anxiety-producing.

· · · · ·

Part of processing our past is to take hurtful experiences and place them into the correct parts of our brain. Thus, the experiences shift from being a painful memory to just being a memory. We are then no longer ashamed of these memories and no longer feel overwhelming pain when we speak about them.

In fact, all the answers are within you and if you've already started sharing stories of your childhood and past hurts, you've already discovered some answers to your challenges. We are a creation of the collective events that we have experienced. You may not have been abused, but maybe you grew up in an environment where emotions were repressed. As a result, there's a possibility that you may have difficulty expressing your emotions in your relationships today, as I did in this next story.

Anxiety and our engagement dinner

When I was engaged back in 2013, my fiancée and I planned an engagement dinner to celebrate with our friends and families. We hosted about 50 guests; half of them were her friends and the other half were mine. The evening was held at a venue located in Gastown and it would be the first time that I would be meeting about twenty of her twenty-five guests. Throughout the entire afternoon, I brooded at home and was very reclusive. I didn't want to talk to her and refused to do anything other than sit on the couch flipping channels on the TV. I couldn't concentrate on anything and I didn't realize at the time why I was brooding. I was short tempered and had tightness in my temples and chest. When she cautiously asked what was bothering me, I closed up and told her *"I'm not in the mood to talk."*

She suspected I might have been feeling nervous about the dinner and gently explained how she was feeling anxious as well in an attempt to soothe my nerves. I didn't acknowledge her because at the time I didn't even realize it was anxiety I was feeling.

From anyone else's perspective this should have been a joyous occasion with true reason to celebrate. Instead I saw it as a death sentence to an evening I was not going to enjoy because I wouldn't know most of her friends and because I disliked small talk with people I wasn't familiar with. It didn't help when she told me about one of her longtime male friends, Mitch, who I had never met before. She explained that he was the type of guy that once would have bullied or given meeker guys a difficult time back in high school. She went on to describe him as a big guy, a biker, but one of the most kind-hearted friends she has. She closed off by saying, "...I can see him liking you...but I can tell you right now that you won't be his best friend..."

As someone who was bullied throughout high school, this sent a flurry of triggers inside of me. Furthermore, she insisted that I give a speech at the dinner to thank all our guests despite my nerves and reluctance.

With my anxiety at a complete high, I started an argument, blaming her for my feelings hours before heading out to the venue.

"Why did you insist on inviting so many people?"

"Do you realize this dinner is going to cost us over $1200 for a mere few hours?"

"What IS an engagement party anyway? Why do WE have to do one?"

"I hate being the centre of attention!"

"I'm not in the mood to go...I hate this idea of yours!"

I continued to rage on about how I didn't want this engagement dinner in the first place and accused her of doing this only to show off to her friends that she's engaged to be married.

Throughout dinner I put on my bravest smile and endured the three hours we had at the venue. When I finally met Mitch, I already had a pre-meditated belief and concluded that he was someone I didn't like. My speech thanking everyone for attending felt awkward and contrived. My notions of the rest her friends were less than favourable and I made all of it clear to my fiancée when we returned home later that night. I once again started an argument and the night ended with us going to bed angry and flustered. My inability to recognize and communicate my anxiety led to unmanaged anger that took away what should have been one of our fondest memories together.

Living with depression

What came with my anxiety, anger, and abuse was a life of solitude and hidden depression because I did not allow my friends to truly get to know me. Although I had friends, not one of them knew anything about my abusive childhood or about my brother's schizophrenia. When they asked, I would give vague responses and immediately try to change the topic.

"How old's your brother? I didn't know you had one," they'd say.

"Oh, he's 7 years older," I'd say. "We don't keep in touch anymore. Oh by the way, are you going to the company Christmas party? I heard that this might be the last year which is really disappointing!"

Intimacy was difficult for me in relationships because my partners had to discover me the hard way. Only through my anger and fits did they have a small window into seeing that I was a man suffering from something more.

I sometimes questioned my life while driving home from work: "is this it? Is this as good as it gets?" or "what else is there?"

Sunday evenings were the worst time for me. By dinner time, I had dropped my son off at his mom's house and the weekend was winding down. I would be alone in the apartment feeling blue that the weekend cycle was ending and the work week was beginning the next day. I would feel unmotivated, unable to sleep, and would pace in the apartment alone until the wee hours of the morning. I even remember going into work at 4 AM at times because I couldn't sleep.

In April 2015, my awareness of my vulnerability allowed me to speak to my family doctor about how I was feeling after the breakup. I went on and explained to her that I needed help beyond the relationship and felt that something wasn't right in my life. I told her that I often felt blue when I came home from work and some Sunday evenings when I was getting ready for work the next day. My doctor listened attentively, took some notes, and gave me a brief questionnaire to fill out. The entire process was quite painless and was very encouraging because I felt that I was taking the first steps towards my healing. In the end, I was diagnosed with mild depression and she went on to explain more about my many unprocessed thoughts from my youth and young adult years. My denial and avoidance of these thoughts repressed many emotions in me resulting in depression.

Depression can lead to a life of solitude, avoidance, difficulty with intimacy, anxiety, rage, and abuse. In men, symptoms of depression often include feelings of irritability, anger, and discouragement.

After my meeting with my family doctor, it all made sense to me. I knew from that point on that I needed to take better care of myself by seeking further help if I was to become a more complete person. I began working hard with several therapists and took an immediate interest in books on abuse, anger, meditation, anxiety, compassion, cognitive behavioural therapy and EMDR (eye motion desensitization reprocessing). Reading helped me understand myself more. The more I worked with my therapists and the more reading I did, the more courage I gained to speak out about who I am because I was becoming more educated. I began to learn that my depression was a symptom of things that I held onto for a long time. The years of holding onto my shame, my silence, and my hurt grew into a form of depression. My counsellor, Anita, once explained it this way: imagine you're a turtle carrying extra weight and burden from your life experiences; once you begin sharing and shedding that burden, you will feel lighter and things will become easier and more manageable. That is exactly what happened to me.

I now realize that I've been living with depression and anxiety for years and perhaps even suffered from these things as a child. I needed to process and normalize them by talking to a professional counsellor. I needed to reorient myself to know that everything I went through growing up no longer needs to be hidden from the world and that

I can be my honest self. By doing that, I can walk taller every day and not feel as though "this is as good as it gets."

Living with depression as an adult without awareness or education about this disorder can be challenging. If you or your partner suffer from depression it requires patience, understanding, compassion, and empathy. It also requires professional help to talk about it, understand the source of it, and to find ways to manage it.

In 2001, the World Health Organization stated that one in four people will be affected by mental disorders at some point in their lives.[8] In Canada, 11% of men and 16% of women will be diagnosed with major depression in their lifetime.[9] However, the key word here is *diagnosed*. Imagine for a moment how many people are wandering around the streets, going to work, playing ball, going to the gym, buying groceries, filling up their cars with gas, and doing other regular activities while suffering from depression without knowing it. Like myself, I didn't know it until I was in my early forties. The actual percentage of those who suffer from depression could be much higher. It's an alarming statistic that certainly needs more attention and education when we are younger to raise early awareness. There are a lot of causes of depression such as genetics, family history of controlling behaviour, drugs, alcohol, sexual abuse, physical abuse, cultural and religious beliefs, socio-economic status, and bullying, to name a few. If we start educating our youth about depression early on, we will be better equipped to manage our challenges as adults.

CHAPTER 4

Making Peace With The Dragon – Taking Action With Tools And Resources For Healing

Taking action involves commitment and patience. It's a crucial part in our healing because if we don't allow ourselves to change, the unhealthy behaviours from our past will eventually repeat themselves and we will be back to square one again. Thus, we need to equip ourselves with tools and to practice using them just like any life skill such as cooking, driving, or using a computer. When we make use of the following healing tools as a regular part of our lives, they become ingrained in us and accessible whenever we feel overwhelmed.

Counselling

I was very fortunate that one of my first counsellors, Anita, was someone with whom I felt safe and comfortable from the start. She was the first person I called after my breakup with my fiancée because I knew she was a dependable resource who could help me on short notice.

Counselling is confidential according to the law, unless you are believed to cause harm to yourself or anyone else. No one may know what is said or who you have spoken to. Counselling services are often free and covered by your company's employee assistance program (EAP). If you don't have an EAP, an hour-long counselling session could range from $80 to $150 in Canada. I agree that it is expensive, but that's also the same cost as a pair of new shoes or clothes if you elect to do some retail therapy instead. Note that the high that our brains reach when we buy something new only has a short lifespan. A session in counselling will last much longer and be an investment in your emotional well-being. There is by far a greater return on investment with counselling than with shopping. In some instances, there are counselling services that are publicly funded and free of charge. For example, I worked with a counsellor named Guillermo who focused on men and abuse. He turned out to be one of my most valuable resources even to this day.

I have gone to many forms of counselling such as anger management workshops, cognitive behaviour therapy (CBT), highly sensitive people (HSP) workshops, and eye motion desensitization reprocessing (EMDR) therapy. EMDR therapists are specialized and research is needed on your part to make sure they have the proper certification and experience. Visit www.emdr.org to find an EMDR therapist near you. All of these sessions and workshops have provided me with powerful tools to help me manage stress. My arsenal of support and what I've learned just keeps getting bigger. I recommend that you research any or all these options as they may also be a fit for you.

Similar to EMDR therapists, not all counsellors are trained in CBT so if you're interested in this type of therapy, it's important to ask them if they are. CBT is about shifting our thoughts. Typically, what happens is an event occurs followed by a thought, followed by a belief, and finally by an action or behaviour.

Here's a simplified example:

I'm stuck in traffic (event). My thought is that there is some asshole who can't drive and causing this traffic jam (thought). I think that it's stupid that the city doesn't put more resources into better highways and to not allow certain people to drive (belief). I honk the horn and start cursing (action). In addition, I call my colleague at work and begin to ream him out for not completing the task that I asked him to do (action).

As you can see, the only thing factual in this example is the event that "I am stuck in traffic." The thought, belief, and actions are based on unproductive assumptions which probably raised my blood pressure. My thought is an instinct that there's someone who can't drive and is deliberately causing the jam. If I'm able to shift that thought into something healthier, I might be able to change that action. What if I thought, "hmmm, I wonder if there's an accident I can't see." My belief then might be, "I hope no one is hurt." Finally, my action might be, "I'll have to wait and find out what has happened. In the meantime there isn't much I can do. Let's see what's on the radio."

Simply catching our initial thoughts and shifting them can have a much different outcome for our actions. Like anything worth attempting, this takes time to learn as our thoughts are so innate they occur almost instantly; yet that's the critical point at which to catch and shift them.

· · · · ·

When seeking a counsellor, take your time and find one that is a good fit. I went to several before choosing the one I now see regularly. Just like a doctor or dentist, it's important that you find one with whom you are comfortable and who understands your needs. When finding one on the phone, ask them questions such as whether they have worked with clients with similar problems. My fiancée at the time and I once went to a marriage counsellor who I did not connect well with. As it turns out, we were the first couple she had worked with.

It's unlikely that one session will be enough. After all, if you'll be sharing your stories just like I have been, it will likely take some time. It's important to be patient with the process. A good counsellor will be compassionate and supportive and most of all will ask some very good and healthy questions to help you reflect and think. In doing so, they may guide you to conclusions that you will discover about your life. Counsellors will not tell you what to do (unless there are immediate sign of danger). They are professionals who will guide you in making your own decisions. Ultimately, that's what you want – to take control of your own life. They will guide you in finding your path of self-discovery and the sources of your problems.

Remember that counselling is your time. Use it however you'd like. I've attended sessions in which I bawled my eyes out about the abuse I faced growing up. I've even expressed extreme anger and cursed my *Ah-Cow's* abusiveness towards me. And I've had sessions where I've been very introspective and even took notes on what I learned and discovered about myself.

Counselling provides a very valuable tool called validation. Validation is a powerful word. The Webster dictionary provides the following definition of validate: *"to recognize, establish, or illustrate the worthiness or legitimacy of."*[10] Validation does not tell us if we are right or wrong. That is not the objective. The objective is to be reminded that we are important enough to be heard without judgement, which is exactly what a good counsellor will do. Validation can bring so much relief to the person venting and a solution will most of the time present itself. Whether it's your teen venting to you about feeling depressed, your wife venting about her job, or your friend venting about family issues, we all need to have that safe space to share our thoughts and be heard.

Society needs to take away the stigma attached when one seeks help from a counsellor. We go to a massage therapist to relieve back pain, a doctor for regular physical exams, and a dentist to check our teeth, so why don't we see a counsellor or psychiatrist regularly as well? I suggested to my friend to go see a counsellor when he and his wife got into another heated argument, and his response was, "we're not quite there yet." The stigma and fear of seeking help and talking about our problems can be overwhelming and daunting but keep in mind that counsellors take no sides and cast no judgement. They are professionals trained to listen and provide useful insight that is less painful than you might think. I go to counselling regularly to have my emotional health checked up. I have told this to my son and he's also worked with a counsellor for years. He's suggested a few times that he needs to see a counsellor after some challenging days. He's even sat in on a session with me.

We need to take care of ourselves both physically and mentally. As life progresses, we have so many contributors to stress such as schoolwork, finances, relationships, parenting, tragedies, and careers. We tend to turn to the nearest watering hole and get plastered with our buddies to forget the stress, rather than entrusting our problems with a professional who can offer life-changing insight, wisdom, tools and resources that will have a much longer lasting effect than what the bartender has to offer.

I mention counselling and therapy first because it's important to seek one-on-one professional help to start the necessary healing. Counsellors can provide you with great tools and exercises in a safe environment, some of which I share with you in Appendix 1. Going to counselling is such a great resource that I can't emphasize its importance enough. Equally important is doing the work you learn from counselling.

Workshops

In addition to counselling, there are many workshops offered on anger management, mental health, and meditation. I once voluntarily attended a three-month workshop on anger management in a dingy, foul smelling office in the heart of Chinatown. At first I was a little reluctant, nervous, and scared because the other participants were mandated by the provincial government to attend for child or spousal abuse. After one session, my judgement of them disappeared and rightfully so; after that, I simply saw them with compassion as men who were also suffering.

One fellow, Steve,[11] told a story about his abuse towards his wife. His story was similar to mine; he was just an average middle-aged citizen who had a difficult time managing his overwhelming emotions and faced challenges dealing with them in a healthy way towards his family. My heart reached out to him because I know his struggles run deeper than the anger he inappropriately took out on his family. He certainly had an unhealthy relationship not only with his wife, but also with his mother which could likely be traced back to his childhood.

Another fellow, Tim, was also abusive to his family but had a harder time acknowledging that his forms of discipline were inappropriate. It turned out that when he was growing up, his father was physically abusive to him and often beat him with similar forms of discipline that made him believe that his methods were acceptable.

There has been immeasurable value in me attending these group workshops as I have shared about my explosive bouts of anger and how I have taken out my anger in my relationships. Listening to other people's stories has helped me see that I am no different than them – we all have issues from our past to deal with. Sharing in a group also provides accountability. It can be easier to talk about your shortcomings to people who have gone through similar challenges and can be more empathetic. The group environment also provides support reminding us that we are not alone with our struggles.

In that workshop, we spent time discussing our family backgrounds and our environment growing up and how they have shaped who we are as adults. We talked about what we didn't know as kids that we blindly carry into adulthood. I listened and actively participated by finding courage to bring the shame put on by my abusers into the open. We went through breathing exercises and techniques for identifying with our feelings.

In one exercise, we began by sharing the words, "I feel (insert feeling)" to help manage and identify the baseline of our anger. Whenever we say, "I FEEL hurt" or "I FEEL humiliated" or "I FEEL scared" we stop blaming the other person and take responsibility for our own feelings and pain. We no longer empower others to control our feelings and we take back that control. When I use "I feel" statements, I am taking accountability and have the opportunity to better understand where my frustrations might have originally come from. The following examples show how these statements can help.

Example #1 of an "I feel" statement

When stuck in traffic, I used to react negatively with, "FUCK traffic! This is so stupid and the driver in front of me shouldn't be on the road!"

However, if I shift that statement internally and say, "I FEEL frustrated that there's a traffic jam right now" I can slow down the unnecessary wave of anger and rationalize my feelings. I might be able to identify some of my past triggers as well.

Possible Origin: My dad often used to curse and blame other drivers for things when he drove. This was modelled behaviour for me when I experience traffic jams. I reacted to traffic the same way my dad used to which was with anger instead of identifying the primary feeling of frustration.

Example #2 of an "I feel" statement

Sometimes when my fiancée didn't text me for an entire day after I left messages I used to wonder if she was mad at me or maybe even ignoring me. Many times I would overreact and text or call her incessantly.

However, if I would have shifted that statement internally and said, "I FEEL scared and insecure when she doesn't text" I could have slowed down my anger and rationalized where the triggers might have been coming from.

Possible Origin: The word love wasn't used when I was growing up. I remember that experience of being thrown out of the house crying and how unwanted I felt. I even remember wanting to run away and no one in the house appearing to care. Being called worthless by my caregivers also contributed to my insecurities as an adult.

Workshops are an excellent way to find healing among others who share similar challenges. Being around others reminds us that we are not alone when it comes to our suffering and that gives us the courage to continue moving towards changing our unhealthy beliefs.

Meditation

I meditate from time to time. There are tons of resources out there on meditation including books, workshops, online videos, and phone apps. Meditation is about being at peace and present. Our minds are constantly filled with thoughts running in all directions about our distant past, our recent past, later on in the day, the next day, or even as far as our death bed. One of the things that meditation is about is getting to know ourselves better on the inside by raising internal awareness of our bodily sensations and our running thoughts. It's about acknowledging all that's going on around us and centering ourselves back in the present. One of the eventual outcomes is that our bodies will relax, our thoughts will be acknowledged, and we will begin to feel more at peace. The irony is that if we use meditation with the intent to take away our pain, it's usually not as successful. But if we shift our mindset and make the intent to simply be aware of our bodily sensations and running thoughts, one of the unexpected outcomes is eventual pain relief.

In addition, when we start feeling sad, depressed, or anxious, we are only hurting ourselves with our thoughts about the past or future events. When we are present, we tune out the busy thoughts in our head and can appreciate the things we are currently doing. Our minds will naturally feel more relaxed and we can appreciate the activity we are doing even more, whether it's reading, sleeping, watching a play or even sitting in traffic.

Some days I have been filled with anxiety on how my work day will turn out, how my son will do at school, or when we were together, why my fiancée was not returning my texts. When we think about future events, our anxieties can come into play and consume us.

When I think of the past and start missing "how good things used to be" or wondering what it would have been like if I didn't move in grade 1, I can start feeling depressed.

As you can see, these are very different feelings, but very powerful ones that can easily determine my actions and behaviours. With the former example of feeling anxious about not receiving a text, I might end up calling my fiancée obsessively until I find out whether she's mad at me or not. And in the latter example of feeling depressed, I might feel like curling up in the darkness of my apartment instead of going for a walk with a friend.

Meditation helps me settle down and focus my mind on the present. It doesn't fight my ongoing thoughts. It acknowledges them and allows them to come and go like a leaf floating down a river. Meditation and breathing go hand-in-hand. In meditation we center ourselves with our breath. The next section looks at what this means.

Breathing exercise

Sit or lie down somewhere comfortable without any distracting noise or light. Gently close your eyes for a moment (after you read this). Take a deep breath in through your nose so you can hear the gentle sound of the inhalation; exhale through your mouth. Feel what's going on in your body starting with your feet all the way to your head (i.e. temperature, pressure in your temple, heart rate). Pause at a spot where you notice some discomfort and be with the sensations of your body for a moment. Once you've gently acknowledged these sensations, let them go and return the focus to your breathing. If your mind wanders (which it will!), gently acknowledge the various thoughts, then let them go and return your focus to your breathing for a few more minutes. Go ahead and try it.

What did you notice and feel in your body? Is there tension in the jaw or temple? Is your chest tight or relaxed? Did you have a lot of wandering thoughts? I usually do and my running thoughts can distract me but I do my best to return my focus to my breathing and what's around me. What did you hear? Likely, you heard the sound of your breathing and maybe even heard some surrounding noises. I can usually identify about three different sounds in the background other than my breath. I can hear the outside wind, the ticking of the living room clock, or the sound of the rain on the deck. How many can you hear?

That's an example of centering yourself to your breath. When we meditate, our mind will wander with thoughts about anything and everything. We center ourselves to our breath to gently draw us back to the present moment when there are no worries, no fears, and no sad thoughts. However, when you're meditating, remember to welcome and acknowledge your bodily sensations and thoughts when they come. Do so gently in your mind, saying to yourself, "I can feel that tingle in my lower back," or "I feel that pulsating in my temples," or "these are just thoughts, it's ok...I know that this is perfectly natural and healthy." By acknowledging our bodily sensations and thoughts, they will naturally float away and you can center yourself with your breath again. Especially to those who experienced physical abuse, your body is an early warning sign to some unhealthy thoughts and actions. For example, tightness in the chest, increased heart rate and pulsating temples can trigger an alarm to be on defense and lead us into waves of anger.

Whenever more thoughts come, continue to acknowledge them in your mind: "It's ok, this is about me being present right now. I know I have a lot of thoughts and worries... just let me take another moment while I breathe." Find words that work for you but remember to acknowledge your thoughts and to ground yourself in your breath. Afterwards, you will likely feel calmer and refreshed.

There was a period of nine months when I meditated every morning for just five minutes before going into work. I continue to meditate whenever I feel like it, have difficulty falling asleep or just need to slow the world down while I appreciate what is around me. Sometimes I meditate even though I'm not feeling overwhelmed at all. It's not only a good practice, but it also helps me heighten my awareness of and appreciate what I already have.

I was recently on a business trip to Denmark visiting a small town called Silkeborg. One evening I sat quietly in my room with the window open, meditating for fifteen minutes, breathing in and out, listening to the beautiful sounds of the small town taking in my wonderful experience being in this charming place. During my trip, I felt a greater appreciation for my experiences and the town because I was more present. I felt the serenity and charm of the town and sucked the marrow out of every experience and moment I had there like sitting outside on a patio, reading, eating a European hotdog, and drinking a beer. I went on hikes and jogs and took in sounds that were foreign, yet comforting. I watched the sun rise and set and noticed the beautiful change in colours of the town. I was very present and loved every experience of that trip.

Do what works for you and always remember that meditation is a tool for you even in heated arguments or situations. I continue to meditate, even at work, in bathroom stalls, or in my parked car. I use it as a tool to simply be present and recognize my bodily discomforts and thoughts. A friend of mine, Joanne, used to gently say to me, "Be still..."

Slow down the pace of your thoughts. I guarantee that regardless of how efficient you are in getting all your thoughts and tasks accomplished, more thoughts will constantly flood your head and will never end. Thus, what difference does it make to quickly get everything accomplished versus taking your time? Things on your to-do list in your head will never be completed. Slow them down, be present, and notice your drive into work or school. Notice the taste and texture of the delicious meals that you prepared. Smell the delicious scent of those baked goods as you walk by the bakery. Listen to the sounds of the morning breeze, the birds, and the kids playing outside.

I have a friend who is good at being present. She hardly demonstrates any worries or anxieties and is a very positive person who is high on life. She's always very focused on what she's presently doing. When she goes away on long holidays, she doesn't pack until the night before she leaves or even until the morning of. Conversely, I have another good friend who often worries about the future. We would plan our summer camping trips and because of the reservation policy we would book three months ahead of time. After we would make the booking, she would often ask incessantly, "Do you think it's going to rain? What should we do if it rains? Oh, I hope it doesn't rain!" In these examples, neither person is getting anything accomplished about the future, except the first friend isn't panicked, worried, or filled with anxious thoughts and can simply go on with her day with much more focus.

An example of an anxious mind

"I've had a lovely and relaxing time off during this past week of writing this book. I'm going back to work in a day and I'm already thinking about what I have to do first. I'll check my emails, voicemails, and I'd better check to see if my shipments arrived on time. Oh, and what should I do if they haven't arrived? Gosh, if they haven't arrived, who should I follow up with? Should I ask the lab personnel? But she doesn't get in until 9 a.m. and I need to know right away. Maybe I can call the suppliers. Do I have their phone numbers? And aren't they in a different time zone? Wait...I need to take care of that document that Sales had requested from me before I went on holidays... shoot! I should check with Pearl to see if Josh is still sneezing today. I'm worried that he's sick again and that he needs me. I can bring him medicine or maybe he wants my company while he's sick. I hope he's wearing a thick sweater and making sure the heater is turned up."

When I am more present, my thoughts might look something like this.

"I've had a lovely and relaxing time off during this past week of writing this book. I'm going back to work tomorrow, but I'm going to savour the moments of this break I have left. Thinking about and anticipating what may or may not happen at work tomorrow isn't going to help. There isn't anything I can do about it now. And besides, things might look differently when I get into work since I left my tasks with a very responsible person. Pearl is a very responsible mother. I'm sure if there were any emergencies, she would have called me right away. Our son is 14 years old now and can take care of himself when he's got a bit of a cold. It's his time with his mom now anyway and right now I'm really enjoying writing this book. I feel very peaceful right now. It's sunny outside and a beautiful afternoon. I can hear the birds chirping and I feel a cool breeze through the window. I'm also feeling a little hungry so I think I'll take a break and prepare something to eat."

Not only was I more present but I was able to self-sooth some worries by recognizing some present events and feelings. I'm actually appreciating what I'm doing right now even more. And you'll notice that I shifted my nervous and anxious thoughts to more rational, present, and non-presumptive ones. It is important not to fight your thoughts and feelings. Acknowledge how you're feeling initially and give that feeling a metaphorical pat on the shoulder. The feeling has done its job and you'll find it easier to shift that thought to one that's more focused on the present. Be present and it will make things much easier to manage stress, change, and challenges.

Exercising

Exercise such as walking, jogging, swimming, or yoga is also a healthy way to manage your emotions. It distracts your mind from ruminating excessively. Ever since I got into the routine of going to a daily boot-camp class at a community center, exercising has become a healthy habit for me. Some mornings I wake up feeling worried about life in general, unmotivated to go to work or to do any household chores, but the moment I start exercising, my worries dissolve quickly. My endorphins are released and any painful emotions I might be having are immediately soothed. In addition, I'm so focused on getting through the exercises that I no longer have the space in my head to be worrying about anything else!

Exercising has become a fun activity for me with so many benefits, both physically and mentally. It may not be a popular activity for many people, but I encourage people to start slowly and it won't be long before you begin to reap the benefits from exercising. Whatever works for you, I encourage you to take action (changing it up sometimes), and stay committed to it.

Reading

Reading is a great way to help us be more self-aware and more knowledgeable about issues relating to abuse, anger, and mental health. Books remind us that we are not alone in our struggles because they open up a world of the challenging experiences others have faced that are similar to ours. Reading allows us to be brave and take accountability for our behaviours. Like one of my counsellors said, "open mind, open spine." It takes a lot of courage to face and acknowledge our own struggles, and reading self-help books is a gateway to foster that. There are plenty of useful exercises in books you can do in the privacy of your own home. I found comfort doing exercises in my own space whether I was at home or in a hotel room when I travelled for work. I saw it as a do-it-yourself method of supporting myself and soon it became a hobby and personal interest of mine to read and apply what I learned.

At the end of this book I have listed several recommended books that are a wealth of information. They're filled with specific details on education and exercises you can do to help you on your journey.

Journalling

Another useful tool for healing is journalling. You don't need to be a good writer or even a neat writer. The wonderful thing about journalling is that you can do it on a computer, on your phone, or on a piece of scrap paper. Maybe it should be called jotting instead. Sentence structure and spelling doesn't matter because it's yours and yours only. You basically just write how you're feeling. It can be a few words, a list, illustrations, or even long stories. Writing is cathartic and it transfers your thoughts from inside your head to outside on paper. It relieves your busy and scrambled thoughts so you can discharge them from your head instead of letting them build up and grow.

A counsellor once suggested that after I write, I can simply tear up the paper and throw it away, symbolizing that I've acknowledged those thoughts and that I'm able to get rid of them. I personally like to keep what I write and sometimes reflect on my changes in feelings, moods, and progress. At times, I've quickly jotted down my feelings on my phone to recognize and acknowledge a difficult time.

When my fiancée first moved out, there was a time when I even tracked my mood hourly and graphed it out to highlight some high and low points in the day. This also helped me acknowledge that I made it successfully through another day and that tomorrow would be a brand new start. This exercise might feel extreme because our feelings are not formulas that can be calculated, but I found it useful nonetheless. It helped me observe my mood and my findings, and allowed me to applaud myself at the end of the day for successfully managing my emotions.

I carried a notebook to work and recorded my feelings when I needed to. When I travelled for work, my notebook was always beside me. Some people may choose something more artistic such as writing poetry, painting, or crafting something. Any of these artistic expressions can be effective and cathartic tools for healing.

Medication

I'd like to touch on medication a little bit in this book. I went on anti-depressants shortly after my fiancée moved out. Although I've never been suicidal, I was clearly feeling blue about something in my life that I couldn't pinpoint that was not just related to my fiancée moving out. I felt it was necessary for me to go on anti-depressants to help me focus while beginning to work with counsellors on my deeper challenges.

If medication is something you think might be helpful in your situation, speak to your doctor about your feelings and difficulties. Your doctor will guide you and make the necessary recommendations. I strongly encourage you to ask lots of questions and do your own research because there are side effects with all anti-depressants, some of which can be very unpleasant and difficult to cope with.

Remember that medication is only a support tool, not a primary one such as counselling and therapy. Regardless of what medication you're on, if you are not committed to seeking professional help and doing the work that goes with it, the medication will not get rid of your problems. It can certainly help you identify and talk more easily about your challenges, but much like a pain killer when you have a headache, it only masks the symptoms so that you can continue on with your day. Medication doesn't heal the root causes of your pain.

I decided to go on anti-depressants alongside my therapy and personal healing. On its own, I can tell you that medication would have done nothing for me except hide the truth from myself. With medication alone, I would have continued to lead a life plagued with the shame that my abusers put on me and I would be in denial of the truth. A year and two months after starting anti-depressants, I spoke to my family doctor and slowly weaned myself off my prescription. I am now doing well without it. The work I've done to date has been very helpful and I am much more in tune and connected to my emotions and feelings. As a friend told me, going off medication "is like taking the crutches off."

However, I want to emphasize that I continue to take action and do the work: I go to counselling, talk about my life with trusted people, exercise regularly, attend workshops, journal regularly, and occasionally review my old notes that I have accumulated through my journey. I talk to my son about my journey from time to time and even to his mom. Should I need and decide to go back on medication, I feel confident and comfortable enough to have that conversation with my family doctor. I also continue doing meditation, staying present, and recognizing any bodily triggers.

Although I'm not in a position to recommend whether or not medication is right for you, it is an option to consider.

I mention it in this book because it has been part of my experience. It is best to check with your family doctor.

Compassion

Over the years, one of the simplest and quickest tools for healing has been learning to give and receive compassion. It's such a powerful word and it's a healing tool we all need. Compassion means to feel suffering together. When our children feel scared during a thunderstorm, we curl up beside them and feel their fears together to help alleviate their worries. When our friends go through a breakup, we listen to them and feel their hurt together. When a loved one passes on, we join together in sorrow. When tragedy strikes the world in the form of terrorism, we reach out together in solidarity and feel the pain of the victims.

Compassion is a healing tool because it validates a person's suffering. A person showing compassion says to one who is suffering, "It's ok to feel (insert feeling)." A compassionate person doesn't question or judge the feeling but instead sits beside the one who needs comfort until the hurt is expressed, processed, and eventually subsides. You feel as though you can turn to that person in times of need. When someone shares your hurt, it immediately builds trust, intimacy, and connection in your relationship and allows you to be vulnerable. And being vulnerable requires a lot of strength and bravery. Thus, when intimacy and trust are built, you no longer need as much courage and it becomes easier to open up to share your feelings with that person. This is also where group counselling is effective because it offers so many compassionate voices.

I have a good friend named Christine who is perhaps the most compassionate person I've ever met. With every message I send her about a difficult moment in my life, I can always rely on her to reply with words of compassion: "I know that breakups are hard," she would say followed by a shared experience. Or she might say, "I know how you feel," "Aw, you must be feeling disappointed," or "You sound really angry and frustrated about your day." Because of her capacity to be compassionate, I'm able to share with her about the toughest times of my life without fear of judgement. And likewise, I feel closer and more connected when she shares a challenge of her own with me.

In contrast, there was a time several years ago when my son refused to speak to me partly due to my abusive behaviour. He refused to speak to me or come to my apartment to see me for a period of eight months. I called him, texted him, and emailed him apologizing and trying to understand where his pain was coming from, but his only replies were short messages of anger and hate. For me, that was an excruciatingly long time given that I've been a regular part of his life despite the divorce from his mom. I was feeling depressed, sad, and anxious as a result, and I decided to go to counselling. I missed him dearly and thought about him every day for those eight months. I missed celebrating his birthday and Christmas with him during that time and I did my best to remain present and smile despite my broken heart. At home, I would sometimes weep just by staring at his photograph. My fiancée at the time would curtly ask, "Why are you crying?" and remark, "I think your son is just being a jerk!" Instead of feeling compassion and building a connection with me, walls were created and trust was broken. Eventually, I pulled further away from sharing my feelings with her about my son and it became a highly sensitive topic to discuss.

· · · · ·

When I openly shared with my friend Christine that I had been abusive towards my fiancée, she naturally said she was disappointed in me. But more importantly, she also said I was very brave and understood the challenging days ahead for me of attending therapy and workshops. My shame lifted when I exposed this truth about myself. I felt disappointed in myself and held myself accountable, and thus could do something about it to make the needed change. Had I held onto my shame, I would not be able to move forward in my healing. I would have continued to build walls, deflect, and take my anger out on others in order to mask my shame. Much like when I was filled with shame about my brother's mental illness and my abusive upbringing, I wouldn't talk about it with anybody and it would get bottled up and released in the form of abusive behaviour. When our lives are weighed down by shame we subconsciously find ways to mask it by turning to self-destructive behaviours such as anger, verbal abuse, alcohol or other substance abuse, promiscuity, resentment, eating disorders, or self-neglect.

Childhood abuse survivors tend not to receive much compassion or empathy from others while growing up. Thus as adults, receiving compassion from others isn't something that is easily accepted. When I was beaten by my dad with a stick and cried alone outside cleaning my socks, I was alone in my suffering with no one to validate the hurt. No one told me it was okay to feel hurt, therefore the last message I heard was, "I am worthless and unlovable."

As adults, we need to show ourselves compassion and remind ourselves that the hurt we carry wasn't our fault. Here are some things to keep in mind about giving, receiving, and accepting compassion.

- We cannot be compassionate towards others until we have self-compassion. This requires that we understand and forgive ourselves.
- We can receive compassion from our counsellors, friends, ministers, teachers, or colleagues. Find someone in your life who is compassionate. When you receive words of compassion, pause for a moment, relish that feeling, and acknowledge how it feels to accept compassion.
- If you don't have someone in your life who is compassionate, use yourself as the voice of compassion. In the book *Becoming the Kind Father,* by Calvin Sandborn, the author uses a tool where he speaks to himself offering compassion when needed. I've used this tool often and it's incredibly effective when we validate our own feelings without judging them.
- And finally, remember that offering compassion does not mean offering solutions. If people want advice, they will ask for it. They usually just want someone to listen and sit beside them with words of kindness during their suffering.

• • • • •

It can take a lifetime to unravel the pain and unhealthy beliefs we have been subjected to. When we talk about our healing, whether it's 20 days or 20 years, the work doesn't necessarily have an end-point. Remember when I said going to a counsellor is like going to a doctor or dentist? Just because I've been to a doctor for 20 years doesn't mean I can now stop going. The choice is there to stop, but what could be the potential consequences? Undoubtedly, it's hard work when it comes to dealing with our past. I embrace and acknowledge that my dedication and healing will need to continue for the rest of my life. Given what I've been through, I don't feel comfortable going on "auto-pilot" and I recognize that I will need to be more mindful of my bodily sensations, running thoughts, and potential triggers.

When I attended a volunteer workshop on men with mental health challenges and issues, I came out with a goal to be recognized as an ambassador for mental health and healing. Although your journey may not guide you there, you may simply want to feel happy and fulfilled for the rest of your life. In the end it will be worthwhile when you think how much you've grown, evolved, and shared with your partner, children, family, and friends. Search and understand yourself and find the real you buried beneath the layers of hurt and suffering that you went through growing up.

CHAPTER 5

The Kind Dragon – Self-Care

One of the first things I did after I realized how much shame I was carrying was to take care of myself. On an airplane, the safety protocol during an emergency is to put the oxygen mask on yourself before helping the person beside you. Similarly, with personal challenges, you must look after yourself first before helping others. How can you offer love, support, and compassion towards others unless you have that for yourself?

My ex-wife, Pearl, challenged me to make a list of positive things about myself. She asked me to write down 10 things. After I did that, she asked me to write 10 more. And finally, another 10. It's a task that's more difficult than you might think, especially if you were put down for all of your inadequacies throughout most of your childhood days.

My list looked like this. "I'm kind, mentally strong, a good father, hardworking, caring and compassionate, thoughtful, gentle, loving, giving/generous, sweet, understanding, accepting, handsome, committed, smart, friendly/nice, responsible, organized, fun loving, funny, peaceful, energetic, spontaneous, adventurous, proud, reliable/dependable, accountable, non-judgemental, brave, dignified, a gentleman, forgiving, open-minded, secure with myself, confident, in control, worthy."

The list grew larger and I would continue adding to it periodically. These were things I started realizing about myself that became my new beliefs and values. Pearl then asked me to commit myself to saying these things out loud in the mirror every day for at least 21 days. Studies have shown that it takes a minimum of 21 days of doing something consecutively before it becomes a habit. I went further than that and did this routinely for six months straight without missing a single day. I said it out loud with conviction in front of the mirror every morning after I woke up. I keep that list near me to this day.

The point of these positive affirmations is to see ourselves in a positive light. When we've been put down so much that we believe these negative thoughts about ourselves, we need to start believing that we are worthy and lovable. Only when we know these positive things about ourselves can we reach out to others with genuine compassion. When these new beliefs become ingrained in our heads they can somewhat unravel what our subconscious has been saying about ourselves all these years. I know that I am friendly and nice and so this becomes one of the beliefs that I hold myself accountable to. And anytime I lash out at someone, I know that I have broken my belief and value of being friendly and nice. When we break our beliefs, we don't feel good about ourselves and know that we need to reset our compass, focus on being present, and start again.

Our beliefs were formed by our caretakers and our environment when we were kids. If we were led to believe that stealing and hurting others was okay, then we will likely still believe this when we grow up. My belief as a child was that abusive and destructive behaviour was tolerated and acceptable. As a result, I carried that belief into my adult years. When I realized the truth and started to rediscover myself, the positive affirmation exercise helped me to recreate the beliefs and values I try to uphold daily. As a result, I can begin to respect and love myself.

Forgiveness, letting go, and acceptance

I've mentioned accountability throughout this book. Ultimately, as adults, we are responsible for our actions and behaviours. Do I choose to lash out at my son for losing his flip-flops? Or shall I choose to be compassionate and remind him that we all lose things from time to time and it's not the end of the world? I've also mentioned that our original abusers created an unhealthy environment that we learned as children; as adults, we must unlearn and retune any of those hurtful and negative behaviours and beliefs.

Although our negative beliefs about ourselves likely started during our childhood, it's important to acknowledge that it is not our caregiver's fault. When we assign blame to the situation, we remain stuck as a victim of abuse. When we remain victims, we externalize our life's misfortunes and give control to the abuse rather than to ourselves. When we are not in the place of understanding or acceptance, then we need to continue to process those memories which takes time. When we don't assign fault anymore to our original abusers, we forgive them for the things they did not know. After all, they likely experienced similar things when they were growing up and regrettably did not have anyone to help them to process their challenges. When we're in a place of acceptance, we're able to speak freely about the past without shame and internal discomfort.

When we assign blame and self-pity due to the unfortunate circumstances of our childhood, we are passively taking digs at our caregivers for their mistakes. We are also making judgements instead of exercising acceptance. We may feel that it's our "given right" to be judgemental of them considering our individual circumstances, however, this is completely misguided. Although nobody had the right to abuse us as kids or adults, the eye-for-an-eye mentality will only keep us stuck in a subconscious mind of blame, shame, and self-victimization.

To this day, I don't really know much about my dad's childhood. I know he was physically abused as a child at a very early age and was responsible for bringing home firewood or there would be no dinner for him - which happened often. One of my counsellors shared that we don't always need to understand in order to accept, which is the case here. I accept that my father had it hard growing up. I accept the reality that I was abused as a child by him. Was it right? Absolutely not. It was certainly unfortunate but I can't change anything about it except to accept it, not assign blame, and to gently remind myself that his abusive actions will no longer define me nor my beliefs. His challenges were his and by no means a reflection of who I was.

Letting go and acceptance takes time. It doesn't happen overnight or at the very moment that we say it. It requires a lot of discussions with your counsellor, trusted friends, and family members, and it takes a lot of self-kindness and forgiveness in order to let go and gain acceptance. Counsellors can help you find ways to let go and free yourself from the burden of resentment and anger. To this day I still work on letting go and finding acceptance because it still hurts from time to time and I sometimes feel anger and resentment towards my original abusers. Yet I also know that exposing the painful stories and feelings by accepting and understanding them with compassion is setting me on the right path towards processing those experiences and healing.

One other thing to note is that it is unrealistic to expect other people to change. They may not have the capacity to change because they may not be at that point in their life's journey and they may never get there. Ironically, once you've focused on your own healing, growth, and self-worth you will find it liberating that you no longer need others to change.

Self-kindness

When we start realizing our self-worth and developing new beliefs, we begin to treat ourselves with much more kindness. We begin accepting ourselves instead of hating ourselves. We soon realize that anger and shaming aren't tools for healing when we're faced with daily challenges. We also learn to peacefully forgive and accept our bad choices from the past.

In my twenties when I lived with my sister, I spent a lot of time going out, particularly with one friend who I really connected with. We went for breakfast, lunch, and dinner quite often. And even though I was working, I look back and realize it was not the best way to spend my money. I insisted on paying for almost all the meals and I some-times picked up some random gifts for her. She felt badly at times, but I insisted. We tried a lot of new and expen-sive restaurants and caught the latest movies together; almost every dollar I earned was spent on meals and activities with this friend. One of the traits of someone who has been abused is that they subconsciously seek other people's approval. Little did I know, my actions were an attempt to seek her approval so she would like me and recognize my worth. I subconsciously needed someone else to see my worth because I couldn't do this for myself.

When I look back, I wish I had been more careful with my money. Some of that could have been saved for my future home, car, or for a rainy day. I certainly made some poor financial choices in my twenties but I also know that it was a confusing time of life for me: I was seeking my identity, friends, and worthiness. During that time I certainly had fun, but if I had a chance to live my twenties over again, I would do things differently. I willfully recognize and acknowledge that was a time of poor choices and understand where they came from.

I am forgiving and compassionate about it. I understand why I went through that phase in my life given what I went through as a child. Whenever we treat ourselves kindly, it helps us to make peace with our past.

• • • • •

Self-kindness is about treating ourselves well mentally and physically. It is about respecting ourselves and setting boundaries. Those of us who went through a difficult childhood may not have received much kindness from our caregivers, the people who should have been the kindest to us of all. If our childhood was filled with kindness from our caregivers, self-kindness will come naturally to us. But if it was not, we need to work much harder to learn how to be kind to ourselves.

At an early age I openly expressed many of my feelings like sadness, love, anger, and hurt. When I did this, I was quickly dismissed by my family members who said I was overly sensitive or too emotional. I always felt as though as I was running against traffic when the rest of the family expressed that I was too sensitive, outspoken, and emotional. There was something suffocating and repressive about the atmosphere in our home because the primary feeling expressed was anger. Smiles and laughter in the household were few and far between.

However, my favourite aunt, Catherina, married to my mother's younger brother, Stephen, was one person in the family who I found I could be a kid around. She was a delightful aunt who always had a big smile for me whenever she came by. She was affectionate and was always laughing and joking around. Her Christmas gifts were the best and included pocket Nintendo games or something a young boy really wanted.

Sadly, my mother was uncomfortable having my aunt around, probably due to my mom's insecurities. My mom would often try to taint my aunt's reputation with me and would attempt to control my relationship with her through guilt and shame. She would often explain how she was victimized by my aunt who "took away" her friends. I would get into arguments with my mom when I defended my aunt. After all, I wasn't prepared to let someone speak poorly about my favourite aunt - a person who made me feel safe and loved. She was one of the few people who I could express myself to and who was good to me. She was the only family member to never scold, lecture, or beat me. She was an angel to me when I was a growing up. I remember her with only happy and pleasant thoughts and I always looked forward to her visits. Even as a young boy, I felt that something wasn't right when my mom would argue with me about someone who treated me with love.

I remember having a high fever one night when my aunt was over for dinner. Her loving words, compassion, and empathy while I lay in bed were lovely, mothering, and nurturing. She was the only member of my family who was always kind to me and left me with fond memories.

Two other people I remember treating me with kindness, love, and respect were my parents' friends, Eddie and Mila. They lived in Seattle, approximately 130 miles south of Vancouver. As a kid, I spent a couple of summers there with their son, Eric. He was a few years younger than me, but we connected and produced some of my fondest childhood memories together.

My aunt Catherina and Eddie and Mila's family all treated me with the utmost kindness and it is through them that I can find kindness within myself.

· · · · ·

Days after my 43rd birthday and after returning from another business trip in Edmonton, I phoned my fiancée to share my feelings with her. I told her I wasn't ready for her to move back in because I was still healing and feeling concerned about having relapses into old thought patterns. This was about a year after she had initially moved out at which point our relationship had been sputtering. I went on to explain what I needed was her support in the form of time, patience, and kindness. An argument somehow ensued and she eventually shouted out of frustration, "This is all YOUR fault!"

I wept on the phone and pleaded that she not say that. She curtly replied, "I'll try...but the truth hurts, doesn't it?"

Shortly after the argument, she finally said goodbye to the relationship and I no longer held onto it either. During my journey of learning about abuse and self-kindness, I realized that I could no longer accept how she was speaking to me anymore, especially in the latter months of the relationship. I understood that she was coming from a place of anger and hurt from the abuse she faced from me. Although she was the one to say that she couldn't be with me anymore, I was thinking the same thing, and we parted ways. I recognized that she needed to go on her own healing journey as I have been doing – and we needed to do this in our separate ways. Self-kindness allowed me to let go and not allow others to cross my boundaries.

• • • • •

Self-kindness and self-care also means that you don't have to harbour anxiety about future events. Feeling anxious hurts your mind which means you are not treating yourself kindly. Instead, take care of your mind. Acknowledge your thoughts and continue to let go and allow them to go along their way. Yoga, meditation, sitting in the bathtub, and sleeping well are all ways to help rejuvenate your mind. Activities such as going for a walk, running, swimming, hiking, gardening, and eating well are all great ways to treat yourself well physically.

It wasn't that long ago when I did no exercise at all. Allow me to back up a bit. When I was in high school, I was typically last in running and the last one chosen for sports. I couldn't wait until I was in Grade 11 when I didn't have to take PE (physical education) anymore.

By my late thirties, I found an inspiring friend who ran in registered runs, enjoyed hiking, and tried new physical activities. I tried doing a few of these things and felt like my lack of physical fitness restricted me. I thoroughly enjoyed being out hiking or swimming at the pool and I wanted to be able to do all these things with less physical strain. I eventually signed up for my first ever 10 km run in 2009; although I gasped to the finish line well after all my peers, I knew it was a goal I wanted to improve on. By setting small goals, I found it more motivating for me to train and to get more fit. I shared my goals with my friends to keep myself accountable and they were all very encouraging. Since then, I've run two half marathons, two sprint triathlons, countless 10 km runs, a 10 km trail race, kayaked, hiked numerous local mountains, participated in the Spartan 5 km relays, and I attend boot camp at the local community center every weekday morning. I swim regularly and bike from time to time; most importantly, I still enjoy my food!

I love what I do and what I've become especially since I was never an active person before. I feel great that I exercise and still do not deny myself one of my favourite foods - hot dogs! I am proud of what I've accomplished and I still have lots of room for dessert. I believe that's being kind to myself.

I encourage you to exercise, but as with everything, start slowly. Go for a walk during your lunch hour or evenings. If you don't have peers to join you, try walking alone. I sometimes find it more refreshing to walk alone because I get to be with my thoughts and process them.

Finding people who inspire you

There is great value in searching for inspiration in others. Your attitude becomes healthier and more positive when you surround yourself with inspiring people.

The friend who inspired me to run was just a beginning runner herself; I found it encouraging to try it since she believed I could do it as well. She started by running shorter distances and was never a strong runner to begin with, but with discipline and training she eventually ran her first marathon in May, 2012. She's a friend who has always believed in me when I've set similar goals. We eventually ran in several 10 km runs together and I found it much easier to have that support. Because of her, I conquered my first half marathon in Victoria in 2012 and I'll never forget her proud smile and embrace of support when I crossed that finish line.

In one of my previous jobs, I had a boss who was brash, controlling, short tempered, and highly critical. He would publicly ream out employees, single people out in meetings, and finger point at the first sign of a mistake. My work days were filled with anxiety, anger, depression, and grief. My home life was a mirror of my days at work and it would be a perpetual cycle. The work environment was toxic for me and I needed to look for a change. I eventually transitioned to a great job at a different company and have a fantastic boss who treats me well and I find inspiration in her. She is understanding about how busy I am at my job, she is patient and compassionate, and she also has a great sense of humour. Because she recognizes my efforts with heartfelt gratitude, I am able to tell her when I've made mistakes at work. She accepts my apology and at the end of the day understands that we're all human and don't deliberately make the wrong choices. Thus, I find motivation to work hard to get results and have no problems working late and on weekends from time to time.

Perhaps my biggest inspiration is my son. When I look at his life and the opportunities he has and doesn't have, I feel motivated to find ways to make sure he grows up in an environment that's loving, understanding, and hopeful. By being able to look at my own childhood and the consequences of my behaviour as an adult, it's much easier to say that I don't want the same things to happen to him. Knowing what I know now about how we learn from the environment we grow up in, I now have the ability to create a much brighter path for him by doing my best to model healthy beliefs and values. And although he still struggles at times emotionally, I know that he's on a better path to healing. We talk about our experiences at counselling and I talk to him about my abusive behaviour in the past. I talk to him about my poor choices and about my upbringing, and I talk to him about my brother and his mental illness. What I want to encourage is an open dialogue where we can share our failures and successes without judgement or fear.

Where can you begin?

You might be wondering where you might begin your journey towards self-discovery. Life isn't linear and there is no step by step procedure to tell you how to live it. However, I guarantee you one thing: your journey will be different from mine and you will find certain steps easier than others. If at some point in your life you feel that something isn't quite on track and feel the courage to self-evaluate to change things up a bit, here's a summary of where I began and what you can do to get things started.

- **Share your story.** This is the most important action you can do on your journey. Expose the true person that you have hidden all your life and talk to someone about your life growing up and how it is today. Share it with a trusted person whether it's a friend, family member, counsellor, member of your church, teacher, or other. Share your story. It's yours to tell and your truth to share. Don't allow others to shame you when you are being your honest self.

- **Be brave.** Allow yourself to be vulnerable. This is critical to your healing and to starting to change your life. Let your emotions flow without judgement. Cry, rage, curse, or smile if you want to. Share your story without sparing any details on how you felt during that time of pain.

- **Find a counsellor to work with.** I looked around a few times to find one that was a good fit for me. Find one who fits your style of conversation, is the gender you're more comfortable with, who's close to work or to home, and one that can fully understand what you're going through. Meet with them regularly. Go to your sessions being brave knowing that they are not there to judge or shame you. Find support groups or a Meetup (a social network that puts together mostly free offline meetings on various interests in different locations) in order to share your story among like-minded people who want to reshape their lives. You'll be surprised by how inspiring their stories will be. This is the most crucial part of healing to help you process your past and to learn acceptance of yourself.

- **Be accountable.** Accept responsibility and the consequences for your own actions. In doing so, you allow yourself to move on without shame. Being accountable also means that you are empowering yourself to spark change and not assign blame to others. Expecting others to change simply means that you are not taking accountability for your life. Be at peace with them. Forgive them for they are not present and aware of the path that they walk on. Be at peace with yourself, acknowledge the choices you made in the past, and move forward knowing you may not have made the healthiest choices and that you understand where those choices came from. Acknowledge and be accountable for your past and share it without judgement. Apologize to those you have hurt without justification and liberate yourself from the anger and shame that you put on others. Be compassionate of their suffering and listen without arguing. This is perhaps the most painful and difficult part of healing and may take a lot of time, patience, and courage. Successfully getting through this step will show that you're on the right track to change.

- **Take action.** Educate yourself and gain a better understanding of yourself by reading, attending workshops, or doing some suggested exercises at home. Other helpful practices include meditation and practicing being present, yoga, exercise, journalling, and joining group discussions. Do these regularly and make them part of your life.

- **Be present.** When you're focused on the now, you will naturally feel a greater sense of peace and happiness and more appreciation for what you have. This takes time to practice, but it's a worthwhile exercise to implement in your daily life. When you are present, your wandering thoughts will subside and you can regain clarity and control of your actions.

- **Practice self-love.** Find ways to recognize your self-worth and be able to see and feel that. When someone gives you a compliment, take it in and pay attention to that tingling feeling inside. That is the feeling you need to give yourself. Write a list of good things about yourself and practice doing some daily affirmations. After a while, you will know them to be true and will walk taller.

- **Connect to others.** As humans we need to connect to at least one person to share our hurt with. Begin with yourself. You need to be self-compassionate to validate the hurt you went through and your courage in doing the work. Once you have self-love you will be able to take in all the compassionate words from others.

- **Be kind to yourself.** Accept yourself for who you are and see yourself in a positive light on your healing journey, regardless of the norms of society or what others may say about you. This is very much like developing confidence. Respect yourself and treat yourself with kindness: exercise, educate your mind, eat well, and indulge once in a while!

- **Find inspiring people.** Find someone who will say to you (not necessarily in words), "I believe in you and you can do anything you put your mind to. I know wherever your journey ends up, you will feel great for trying." They will also be the people who will keep you motivated throughout your journey whether through their words or just by spending time with them.

- **Be patient.** I can't stress enough that your journey will go on for a very long time; I see that as a positive and exciting adventure! Take the time to acknowledge the changes inside of you because you will feel them. You will feel liberated because your past is no longer controlling you. And you will reshape your beliefs from your past and create a new and uplifted version of yourself who will exercise a healthier inner relationship, one with healthier thoughts and actions. I'm excited that my journey will last until the day I pass on. This not only gives me added purpose and meaning, but it feels great knowing I will be a healthier person in my future relationships.

CHAPTER 6

Lessons Learned

Through my journey I've learned to accept that everyone goes through mental health challenges at some point in their lives - some more than others. No one is immune to these challenges, and that has helped me to accept myself. We have all felt hurt and suffering at some point in our lives and these experiences affect who we are today.

Talking about our mental health is something we need to normalize in order to make it easier to reach out for help. It is much like having diabetes, heart disease, breast cancer, or even getting divorced. These are all arguably more accepted in society, making it easier to talk about them and reach out for help. Because there's still so much fear, shame, and stigma attached to mental health we are not quite at a place in society of welcoming it into our everyday lives with acceptance. Instead of being called "abnormal," "crazy," or "schizo" for needing help, we can begin to remove labels and it will be easier to get support. During my youth and into my twenties and thirties, I remember blaming my brother and labelling him for his illness. My mom would plead tearfully to me, "He can't help it, Jay!"

I could not have been more wrong in blaming him. My mom was right – nobody chooses to be mentally unwell.

· · · · ·

We can't always choose our challenges, but we can choose how we deal with them or let them affect us. After my last failed relationship, I could have easily chosen to walk away blaming my fiancée at the time, not look at myself in the mirror, not take accountability, and to go on to my next relationship no better than before. If I had done this, I would likely end up with one failed abusive relationship after another, or living my life alone, miserable, depressed, and helpless while my son follows me down the same path.

Although being brave and courageous isn't easy, it's rewarding to know I am capable of change and I can become a person with a healthier mindset not driven by fear. I have acknowledged how abusive I was in my past relationships. After educating myself about abuse, I am afraid to go down that road again. I feel frightened to know I am capable of hurting my son, my partner, my family, my friends, and myself. These reminders motivate me to excel in my healing and drive me to change.

After I came to the realization that I had been abusive, I wished I could have sat in a conference room and answered any questions from friends, family members, and people I knew. I wanted to take accountability and I did not want to hide from my shame and mistakes because that only creates built up shame, suppressed anger, and explosive behaviours.

Finding support and encouragement

I have sometimes found support in the least expected places. I have chosen a healthier environment for my own sake and the sake of my son. My friends are supportive, encouraging, and caring people who are non-judgemental and not filled with resentment.

I remain friends with a family who I met through my former fiancée and who know about my abusive past. I am deeply moved by their kindness towards me and how supportive they are in my recovery and healing journey. They could have been the least likely to show support given how close they are with my ex, but nonetheless, their non-judgemental actions remind me to be accountable for my healing. I sometimes see them at the park or at the supermarket with their two beautiful kids and each time I receive hugs and warm smiles from them. These actions say to me to "keep going, keep working, and keep being brave."

Although I'm not surprised that my coworkers have been supportive, it certainly wasn't expected. My colleague, Catherine, and I sometimes take walks during the lunch hour and she listens to me with compassion as I talk about my suffering and what I plan to do about it. Her calm voice of reason has provided me with a trusting and safe environment in which I can share my personal struggles. Similarly, from time to time my boss asks me how things are at home and I share about some of my challenges. She is such an incredible woman. She didn't cast judgement on me when I sat down and told her how abusive I was in my relationships. Instead she offered an experience of her own that related to my challenges, demonstrating her compassion, empathy, and encouragement to me to seek support.

My longtime friend who is like a father figure to me, Rene, has been such a compassionate and deeply grounded friend. On a quiet and calm morning during a recent camping trip, he sat on a log alone watching the birds fly by. I sat beside him and we talked in the way I wish I could have spoken to my father. I shared with him about my journey and he listened and then recounted his. Neither of us gave advice, we simply found peace and healing in our sharing. Sometimes the fewest words spoken are the ones that resonate the most.

Finally, I have found support in my ex-wife, Pearl. She has been a source of encouragement on my journey and has provided me with feedback on the changes that she's seen in me. Her encouragement made it possible for me to share my story. I trust that my courage in sharing how abusive I was to her in the past has also been very healing for her.

Changing old ways

I have learned that our parents and caregivers raised us given what they knew from how they grew up. They thought they were doing what was best even when they were using harsh methods to punish us. But unless someone in the family line breaks that chain and shifts the unhealthy beliefs and behaviours, the abuse will continue on in the next generation and so on. How our parents were raised *may* have worked and been effective for them during their childhood, although I would argue there could have been healthier options. But the environment they grew up in, culture and lifestyle, number of family members, and level of affluence all contributed to the decisions their parents made in raising them. And your parents' parents had the same challenges and so on and so forth. Thus, when we put things into context, we can understand the hardships they faced growing up without assigning blame.

Once we can accept that our parents raised us the best they knew how, it becomes easier for us to forgive them. They may not have made the healthiest choices, but they had to make decisions based on what they knew and believed.

· · · · ·

At work there are people who have been doing their jobs for over 20 years and whenever someone asks them to do their job differently, their go-to answer is typically, "it's always been done that way!" Although that's true and possibly effective, doing things the same way because it's been like that for a long time doesn't mean that it's right. If our mind is fixated on keeping things the same, there would be no progress. Imagine no microwaves, computers, television, electric cars, or cell phones, to name a few recent examples of change and progress.

I have learned that change is the only way to healing - and not just change for a day or a week. Being committed to a paradigm shift frees me from my subconscious and from what I was taught to believe. By being flexible and allowing change to happen, I am able to learn. If I shut down new ideas and beliefs, I wouldn't be able to learn and grow.

Feeling happy

I used to compare my life with those of my friends and colleagues. Why is it that they can afford a large home, multiple cars, have a beautiful partner and family, take family vacations and maybe even have a more gratifying job? Now when I remind myself of my self-worth and when I am more present, I realize how tremendously happy I am. I have a great job that allows me to travel and see the rest of Canada and parts of Europe and the US, I have an incredibly brave and intelligent son, I have many incredibly supportive friends, and I have a place I call home every night.

By being present, I can easily see and appreciate all that I have and stop comparing myself to others and their success. Sadly, society typically measures success by the amount of wealth we have. Like my past beliefs, I have chosen to try to shed that standard of success and instead measure it by my own well-being and inner glory.

Sometimes I hear people say that they want to be happy in their life which implies that they aren't presently. For those looking outwardly to find lasting happiness, you won't find it in a new pair of shoes, a bottle of wine or a vacation getaway. After you've received all the compliments on your new shoes, the last drop of alcohol has worn off or you've received the bill for that vacation, what you thought was happiness will merely be added to your piling list of unhappy thoughts.

Much like falling in love, you'll know when you're happy. The feeling, like all other feelings, will come to you when you are prepared to receive it. And you will be prepared to receive it when your mind is in a healthier place and when you have been able to process parts of your past that have been troubling you. When we have the courage to heal that inner relationship with ourselves, we no longer need to look outwardly to find happiness. Then the vacations and new shoes simply become the cherry-on-top to our happy lives.

No matter how well I keep up with the Jones', if I'm not focused on my own healing and well-being, I'll never find happiness. If I am forever comparing myself with my peers and colleagues, I will let what I don't have determine my level of happiness rather than what I have.

Lately I've been able to appreciate my life more and remain more focused on the present. I sometimes still have worries about the future and thoughts about how sad I feel about past relationships, but I acknowledge those feelings and re-center myself to the present and I am easily able to be in a happier state.

A Positivity exercise

List some positive things in your life you are thankful for. After jotting down at least 10 ideas, take a moment to go through each item and reflect a little on how truly thankful you are for it and why.

Here's a list of 10 things I'm thankful for:

- A job that allows me to travel (I get to see parts of Canada, Europe, and the US that I would otherwise never have been able to see.)
- A great son (I feel so delighted and uplifted when we spend time together. I feel connected and hopeful for a lifelong friendship.)
- A healthy relationship with my ex-wife (It's nice to have her over for dinner once in a while to chat about our projects and laugh about our stories.)
- A place to call home every night (My home is warm, quiet, and comfortable. It's perfect for me.)
- Wonderful friends - Vincent, Sandra, Christine, and Rene to name a few (It's always nice to go out with them for dinner or drinks. They're kind, funny, intelligent, and silly.)
- The beautiful province in Canada in which I live (There are lakes, mountains, and shopping nearby!)
- Hot dogs! (If I was trapped on an island, I could survive on hot-dogs.)

- My ability to exercise almost every day (I'm thankful that I can run, walk, and lift weights.)
- My cat Inori (She's so gentle and loving and sleeps beside me almost every night.)
- My sense of humour (knock, knock...ok maybe I'm not that funny!)

Cultural shaming

In Chinese culture, the dragon is a fierce and powerful creature filled with deceit and anger. It is used as a metaphor to describe someone's raging personality, and unfortunately it can be revered in the culture. Whether your culture is Chinese, Iranian, Italian, Irish, Korean, or North American, it really doesn't matter. What's important is to realize how cultural traditions can add an extra piece of complexity to your healing. Webster's dictionary defines "tradition" as: "an inherited, established, or customary pattern of thought, action, or behavior (such as a religious practice or a social custom)."[12]

Tradition can be a beautiful thing because it can give someone a sense of rootedness and identity, often leading to wonder and curiosity about other cultures. In the traditional Chinese wedding and tea ceremony, newlyweds offer a cup of tea to the parents and honour them with words of kindness, respect, and love. In exchange, the parents offer the newlyweds a red envelope that contains money to show their gratitude and to wish them good fortune.

While cultural tradition offers healthy and beautiful customs such as the tea ceremony, some families can take traditions out of context which becomes problematic. For example, in some cultures, parents feel ashamed if their sons and daughters marry outside their culture. This can result in public shaming; in some rare cases, families have gone to the extent of committing crimes to prevent the marriage from happening. Another example is if a son doesn't take on the responsibility of the family business, he may be shunned and possibly disowned by the rest of the family. In other words, family shame will be cast upon the household and generations to come unless the children are obedient and respectful according to the rules of the tradition. Often, families will demand righteousness. However, little do they realize that they are confusing respect with subservience, which have two entirely different meanings. Respect means to admire someone or something that is good and valuable. Subservience means being willing to obey someone and being treated as less important than something or someone else.

· · · · ·

Hierarchies are the ways many traditions have structured themselves and ordered society. Men are the household leaders in making decisions for the family while women and children must abide by the rules made. In many cultures, men are not supposed to express emotions because emotions are seen to be weak and the culture dictates that men need to be strong for the family. But, the true connection is really between strength and feelings. Weakness is when we don't express our feelings in a healthy way. Strength is when we can talk about our feelings and listen to others talk about their emotions.

Think about how emotions are expressed in this example: Your child does poorly in their piano recital.

Option 1: Lecture and yell at them on how they failed because they were lazy, uncommitted, stupid, and useless. Don't allow them the opportunity to express themselves because no good can come of it.

Option 2: Sit down and talk to them to understand why they didn't do so well. Listen to their feelings because there's likely something bothering them that you might be able to help them through.

As you can see in both approaches, the objective of providing what is best for your child is the same. Many cultural approaches would say Option 1 is easier and more effective because the parents are in control of the situation (by raising fear and stating their parental opinion). However, Option 2 is the healthier approach because it demonstrates strength by talking about feelings and listening to your child.

Option 1 is a harmful and unhealthy approach because it projects the parents' own guilt onto their children. They might claim that they just want what's best for their child, which is a noble goal, however, Option 2 also has the same goal so this argument is negated. The reality of Option 1 is that parents often feel judged by their peers and family members based on how successful their children are. However, little do they know their reaction is based on their own insecurities that they may not be aware of or understand. Societal comparisons can be devastating because they blind us to what our true objective of parenting should be: to allow our children to thrive and succeed based on their own strengths.

Guilting

Guilting is a form of control and manipulation. It's a passive aggressive tool used to get someone to do what you want. Again, just because that's how things were done in the past doesn't mean that it's correct. Interracial relationships are healthy and beautiful. Being gay and openly sharing that without judgement is healthy and natural. These are the type of truths that some people deny themselves because of what their caregivers and partners want based on their own insecurities. Guilting is an exchange of goods or services that is conditional and typically followed by an imperative word such as "should." The word "should" is used as a way to control another person and get them to do what you want. It relinquishes the recipient of their own will, freedom, and right to choose what they desire to do. Using the word "should" to fulfill needs can be a form of emotional abuse because it takes away the other person's belief that they are able to make their own decisions and it empowers authority to the person making the demands. For example, some parents might use the following guilting and controlling statements that can be viewed as emotionally abusive.

"You don't love me anymore if you marry him. You should think about that!"

"I raised you all by myself and gave you life...you should be living with me and looking after me now!"

"I supported you through school and cooked and cleaned for you all your life...you should give something back!"

"You should lose weight because no one will be attracted to you!"

"You should listen to what I say because I want what's best for you!"

True love isn't measured by how much you allow others to control you. If you continue to appease others based on their demands, you will find yourself perpetually trapped in their guilting. As a result you may find it difficult to find your own voice and identity in life. In fact, by empowering yourself to fulfill your needs, you are demonstrating a greater love for others by encouraging them to find their own path to healing and be responsible for their own lives. I encourage you to carefully examine your life and determine when you have experienced guilting or have been the one to inflict guilt upon others.

Breaking the chain of fear and control

How does one break the chain of unhealthy patterns being passed from one generation to the next often without awareness of these patterns? We live our lives routinely most days and are set on auto-pilot. Sometimes a life transition can help you look inwards. A life transition might be something like divorce, a loss in the family, or losing a job. Sometimes observing a peer or colleague going through their personal struggles can help you self-evaluate.

Other ways to raise self-awareness include reading self-help books, talking to a counsellor to have a general discussion about your life, or simply looking at your surroundings. If you commonly think things such as, "she was being a bitch at work," or "there wouldn't be any problems if only he did his job," or "my life is unhappy because of all the negative people around me," take a moment to stop these thoughts and self-evaluate.

One day I was feeling a little off at work. A coworker was working on a project that I was tasked with and he was beginning to get a lot of positive results with his work. I felt annoyed that day and kept saying things in my head like, "he's not a team player," "I hope he fails," "he doesn't know what he's doing," and "he's not very good at following directions."

Then I took a step back and dug deeper. I recognized that I felt tightness in my chest and was feeling overwhelmed throughout the day and not my usual self. Later that evening, I journalled all my thoughts. When I self-evaluated, here's what I came up with: I felt insecure and worried my colleagues would appreciate him more than me; I felt scared that my role would be diminished; I felt stupid and inadequate; I felt weak; and because I lacked control of him and what he was doing, my anxiety kept fueling my inner anger. Finally, I felt unimportant.

Notice what happened when I self-evaluated? When I sought to blame him for all the negative things, I no longer took accountability or had control of my feelings. His work and performance dictated how I felt and I was negative and resentful. When I wrote down all my true feelings, I took accountability and discovered that it was all about my weakness, my need to control the situation, and my insecurity. All of this was fueled by my training in my younger years to be fearful, scared, and insecure with myself. Once I drew that connection, it was easier for me to accept the truth that he was only doing his job and doing it very well, and I was part of the problem and not contributing to the movement of that project. In fact, my negativity would have potentially slowed the project down.

· · · · ·

Control is a hidden behaviour that many people struggle to acknowledge. Our caregivers guided us as best they could, but they unknowingly instilled fears based on their own beliefs. For example, "don't go near the lake" may cause us to be fearful of swimming when we grow up, or "homeless people are all losers and drug addicts" makes us fearful and judgemental of people living on the streets. We take these fears, they become ingrained in our belief system, and we end up passing them on to our partners and children. Take a moment to look at some of your beliefs and objectively determine whether they are factual. How have these controlling beliefs affected your behaviours? Then ask yourself where these beliefs originated.

For example, some myths I was taught are as follows:

- Don't look at panhandlers in the eye because they are dangerous.

- Don't play with the neighbour's kids because they are bad.
- All kids who smoke are bad kids.
- Rock music is for bad kids.

These beliefs encouraged the following feelings and perspectives: lack of trust, judgement, fear, superiority, and pessimism. These are all unhealthy ways of looking at the world and these controlling thoughts that were programmed into my subconscious have been harmful to me and my relationships.

· · · · ·

In my previous job I was a manager in a demanding and time-starved environment. My days would start at 6 a.m. not because I had to but because I chose to. I felt I needed to be at work before everyone else so I could get a head start on incessantly responding to all the emails and making key decisions for the department. My actions didn't allow for any creativity from other team members because I demanded creative control. At the time, I didn't realize this because I simply thought I was a good leader who filtered the team from the noise from upper management. The deep-down truth is that I was insecure and fearful of change. I was afraid that someone would make a decision that was different than what I had in mind and I wasn't prepared to make that mental adjustment. I was often furious if someone went against the grain of my decisions because it implied that my knowledge or skills weren't good enough. My false sense of control and fear of change limited my growth and learning.

Our subconscious

Growing up, the following phrases echoed repeatedly in my mind as a result of being abused and bullied.

- "You can't do that!"
- "Shut up and do as you're told!"
- "You're useless!"
- "You're so fucking ugly!"
- "Loser!"
- "Keep quiet and stop playing! All you ever do is play!"
- "Be good or you'll be punished!"
- "You deserved that!"
- "You're the worst one of the kids!"
- "You're too emotional!"
- "Stop being a baby...stop your crying! Boys don't cry!"
- "Get over it!"
- "Shame on you!"
- "That's stupid!"
- "You look stupid!"
- "You should listen to what I say!"

The belief that I'm inadequate was ingrained in my subconscious. Therefore as an adult, my behaviour was the result of attempting to fight back against this subconscious belief in the form of anger, shaming, and abuse.

A good metaphor to use is an iceberg. On the surface, we see a big chunk of ice floating on top of the water which represents our conscious beliefs. However, underneath the surface and unseen is a massive piece of ice that dwarfs the top piece in size. That bottom piece of ice represents our subconscious beliefs. Some examples of our subconscious beliefs might be "I'm not worthy," "I'm not good enough," or "No one's going to accept me or like me."

When we have the capacity within ourselves to begin to look at our subconscious (I realize this is a bit of a paradox), we can support the necessary change in ourselves. As seen in this example, our thought patterns are made up from our belief system.

Think about how you might respond in the following scenario.

Your friend is going to meet you for coffee at 8:30 a.m. at a local coffee shop. You get there at 8:25 a.m. and sit and wait. However, your friend texts you at 8:40 a.m. and apologizes that he isn't able to make it after all.

Scenario A:

My initial thoughts might be

- "What the fuck? What a waste of my time!"
- "I'm so fuckn' pissed off at him for making me wait."
- "He's got some issues...he's always late, he's always disrespectful and he always does this."
- "I'm never hanging out with him again."

As you can see, I externalize my thoughts and behaviours. I lash out and blame others for my feelings of disappointment. My unprocessed subconscious takes the form of anger and shame.

If I dig deeper, my subconscious beliefs (the bottom part of the iceberg) are probably telling me the following.

- I'm not worth his time.
- I'm not likeable.
- He found other/better plans than me.
- I deserved that.
- I feel ashamed.

However, what if my belief system was different? What if I was raised in a household filled with love and understanding? My response might look something like this.

Scenario B:

My initial thoughts might be

- "I hope he's ok."
- "I wonder if there's anything I can do to help."
- "That's ok, we'll hang out another time."
- "I'll just enjoy my coffee and newspaper now."

My subconscious beliefs are probably telling me the following.

- I feel good enough about myself. This isn't about me.

- I don't know why he cancelled. I'm sure he had his reasons and I won't take it personally.
- I like this time with myself right now anyway.

The point is for us to identify what our subconscious is telling us and to address it. Until we can shift the sub-conscious messages our brains have been programmed to know, we cannot experience real change. When we properly process these beliefs, we are no longer stuck in a child's mind fearing the effects but rather we have moved forward in an adult state of mind.

Take some time to reflect on your childhood. Ask yourself about your upbringing, your parents/caregivers and what belief systems they used to raise you. Did they believe in their way only? Did they have an open mind? Were you taught to listen only and not speak? Did they listen and value your opinions? Did they put you down and yell at you to get their message across? Or did they speak to you with respect and kindness?

Reframing our subconscious beliefs is challenging and daunting and may take a lifetime. It is my personal goal to untangle what I learned growing up. It takes courage, bravery, and strength to openly talk about it and take accountability for my shortcomings. It also takes work with professional therapists and plenty of self-reflection with acceptance and without blame. However daunting it may be, I feel more liberated today than ever before now that I understand more about my subconscious. My true self is starting to form where love, compassion, and understanding can drive my life.

• • • • •

When we begin to break these unhealthy cycles, we can view the world with more optimism and begin to feel good about ourselves, almost like being in a new skin. Learning new skills and ideas becomes possible when we can adapt to change. Letting go of control and the need to be doing things "our way" paves the way for many wonderful opportunities. We breathe in the world as it is with acceptance and develop a good, healthy relationship with ourselves.

CHAPTER 7

Finding Purpose

As my healing continues, I have had insights that I wasn't even looking for. I now understand that my son's struggles are a reflection of my own personal struggles. My lack of compassion and patience towards him in the past is ultimately reflected back at myself. When I cursed in traffic or snapped at my mom on the phone in front of him, it's natural for him to take those things from me and believe them to be acceptable behaviours. I realize that my journey of healing provides him with a clearer option for his own future.

When I began to share with him about my abusiveness and that I was attending an anger management workshop and counselling, I did not judge myself but instead explained to him that these are resources to help me get through tougher times. I asked him to join me in my session with my therapist one time and he sat there as a spectator and observed how simple it was to talk to a counsellor. Thus, he was able to see a counsellor without judgement, stigma, or fear. I applaud him for his bravery in having an open mind despite going through some challenges of his own at such an early age. And by observing the shift in my behaviour and mindset, he can finally have a healthy and supportive male role model in his life. He can learn from my mistakes and from my courage. He can always reference his father as someone who failed and succeeded as a source of inspiration.

If he is fortunate enough to have kids of his own someday, he will be better equipped to raise them with a healthy approach to parenting. He can start his family on the right foot and model patience, love, and compassion. If nothing else, perhaps my experience can remind him that that even parents and caregivers are human and can make mistakes from time to time. The true test is in how we address these mistakes and learn from them so we don't repeatedly make them.

I also hope he understands that happiness is something we choose. Just like I have learned, we have a choice in how we respond to an event in terms of our thoughts and beliefs, which ultimately creates our feelings and actions. Our negative perceptions of things can be reshaped into positive ones.

• • • • •

I sometimes cringe when I hear my friends recount their own personal challenges with partners or children. I struggle with discomfort because I can sometimes see my abusive self from my past inside their words and behaviours. Although I share my thoughts with them I know that in the end it is up to them to find the bravery to be vulnerable, to acknowledge their own unhealthy beliefs, and to have the desire and motivation to change.

I sometimes hear my friends speak and use imperatives such as:

"She should be listening to this,"

"I let her do things her way," or

"She should be more (fill in the blank with a behaviour)."

When I hear their stories, what I now hear are words of control, insecurity, shame, and abuse. In some instances, from what I know of their families growing up, they too have gone through a childhood filled with shame, guilt, and harsh discipline. Unfortunately, the argument to obey your parents (unconditionally) and to do what you're told is something that can be so ingrained.

Parents are supposed to be our teachers, caregivers, leaders, and guides. But unhealthy forms of discipline are damaging and repressive to who we truly are. One of my hopes in sharing my story is I will facilitate change in my peers to help them find the courage to liberate themselves and mend any of their hurt relationships.

After my fiancée and I broke up, I called my sister and told her that I am getting help for my abusiveness and that I'm going to be okay. She texted back to say, "I hope to someday find the courage to deal with my ghosts. Remember, I grew up in the same household." It was incredibly brave of her to share that with me. We haven't spoken a great deal since then, but I keep hoping that someday she will find the courage and bravery to be vulnerable and begin her journey towards wholeness. After all she's been through, she deserves that liberation.

. . . . .

It's sometimes difficult to see our previous intimate relationships as having any meaning or purpose. I believe each one has a purpose and offers lessons to be learned. Not lessons such as "I learned that I'm too nice" or "I learned that I need someone more loving and kind." I'm not talking about passive ways of saying that you were too good for that relationship. I'm talking about positive lessons the person has taught you. My ex-wife Pearl would sometimes say to me, "thanks to you, I've learned to be much more organized in my life, not to hoard, and to be more present."

Pearl has taught me an abundance of lessons and has encouraged me to be the better man who she believes exists. When she left me, she said, "I believe in you...I see so much potential in you." At the time, they were just words, but now what I hear are much needed words of encouragement.

Now in my forties, I am starting to see the potential she was talking about. I have learned that I am a more self-aware and centred person than I was during our relationship. For years, I didn't know what that person looked like. I thought I did until my last failed relationship which sparked a much needed re-examination of myself. During the relationship, I tried hard to look at and improve myself and it certainly was challenging with many failed attempts ending in a string of arguments and abuse by me. But after the relationship ended I realized it was a journey I needed to go through on my own and one that she could no longer be a part of, as painful as it was. I needed solace and space to work on myself. Much like skiing, it's hard to learn to do it alongside somebody holding you...you need to do it on your own with guidance from a distance.

From my last relationship, I began to learn the value of counselling, talking, opening up, being vulnerable, and being accountable for my actions. Although I wasn't successful in doing these things during our relationship, I deeply value the takeaways from that relationship and pursue them with passion, motivation, and drive. And although I couldn't see it at the time, she made me see in more ways than one that I needed help. She was the first person I could talk to about my brother and the abuse after forty years of silence. I believe the purpose of that relationship for me was to find ways to begin my healing, to support my son, and to break the chain of abuse. Now I believe my purpose is to take that ball and run with it, and inspire others along their journey.

Whether with family members or friends, we can find purpose in all our relationships. I now accept that my brother has schizophrenia and through that I hope to find the courage to reach out to him someday. I believe that my journey in healing from my abuse, depression, and my better understanding of mental health is guiding me in the right direction. I also find great meaning in my father's life. Despite his weaknesses and mistakes, I no longer seek to blame him but have learned compassion, under-standing, acceptance, and accountability for my actions through him. I've also learned from relationships with my colleagues in my current job. I work with such wonderful people who demonstrate a strong work ethic, kindness, generosity, patience, and respect. I would have no place among them had I continued to carry out my abusive atti-tudes and aggressive behaviours from my past.

In the rapid pace of our lives, it's often easy to take these meaningful experiences for granted. In peaceful moments of solitude, I like to reflect on how fortunate and blessed I am in my life. I'm not a man filled with desire for monetary wealth and outer glory. I find the riches of learning about myself and my purpose in life much more fulfilling than material goods because I can now begin to see myself as having self-worth and being capable of love. I smile when I think about my purpose. It provides me with a target in life to work towards. How I get there is up to me and not driven by the shame of my youth filled with angst, fear, and anxiety.

What will your purpose be? That is for you to discover; you might find it in time if you choose to look for it. I believe my healing is to guide my son. I hope my healing will educate me more on mental health and be supportive of every one of us who is fractured by mental illness in some capacity. I believe my 15 000 days of shame, abuse, anger, depression, hurt, and guilt were all necessary to get me to this point. No one deliberately gave me an abusive childhood but it happened by life's circumstances beyond anyone's control or understanding.

Slowing my life down has also helped me find clarity in my goals. Appreciating what's around me and what I have rather than focusing on what I don't have has been an important part of my happiness. Do I wish for a million dollars and a nice waterfront cottage? Not really. I don't wish for one. But if the opportunity presented itself to me, I certainly wouldn't turn it away. I choose not to live my life chasing after dreams but rather by receiving what comes my way and taking these opportunities to carve out my future.

I encourage you to slow down your thoughts because it will help you find your purpose or purposes in life. My fiancée used to say lovingly to me each weekend morning, "why can't you just lie in bed here with me with our coffee and just enjoy this time?" My anxiety and unnecessary need to get out of bed to start fulfilling future tasks handicapped me from enjoying one of my fondest pastimes with her.

Enjoy your time with your kids, your partner, your friends, and family. You will find the mental weight that you carry will lighten. Why do we take vacations? We do this to get away from our daily stress and to slow things down. When you think about it, we don't really need to go away in order to do that. It certainly enhances the experience, but slowing down is a practice that can be applied in our daily lives at home and at work.

My counsellor, Guillermo, believes that our healing is strengthened by connections. Whether with a friend, family member, or counsellor, we find healing when we connect with someone who understands us and we typically feel better afterwards. And remember to also celebrate your successes. We tend to forget about how great life is and fail to focus on the positive energy that surrounds us. Positive reinforcement keeps us encouraged and motivated and keeps your hard work going. Sometimes after a good meeting with his counsellor, I will take my son out for a nice meal to celebrate, or we might do something fun such as go to a movie and stuff our faces with popcorn.

Just remember that your purposes are for you to unravel and discover. No one can direct you and say you "should" go down a certain path. At one point when I was struggling, I told my mom I was going to therapy and she quickly offered a solution with good intent, "I think you should meditate."

I immediately interrupted and kindly said, "Mom, I can decide for myself, alright?"

She was right, of course, but at the time I wasn't prepared for meditative practice until I addressed other more pressing concerns such as acknowledgement and accountability.

Ultimately you must make your own decisions based on what you need rather than letting others tell you what is best for you. It's up to you to carve out your own future which is an exciting adventure. Remember that you are never alone. At the very least, you have yourself, your own voice, your own friendship, your self-love, self-kindness, and self-compassion.

CHAPTER 8

The Dragon Inside
– My Life Today

I go to the gym every weekday morning for a drop-in boot camp class. Over the years I've met some wonderful people. When I started going, years ago, I was very shy and reserved. But eventually I got comfortable with everyone and now I enjoy myself even more. Going to boot camp has become a healthy start to my day as well as a social function for me at 6 a.m. every day. I made some friends with whom I connect very well. Rob, who is physically fit in his fifties, has been an inspiring friend. I can only hope I'll be as physically and emotionally healthy as he is when I'm in my fifties. We've done some long distance runs together and he continues to motivate me with his positive outlook on life. He ran his first ever half marathon a few spring seasons ago and I was astounded by his commitment and hard work. Rob is a true gentleman who I look up to. Another friend, Candice, has also been an inspiration to me with her dedication and perseverance. She works extremely hard at multiple jobs and still manages to find time to join us at the gym every weekday morning. It's been challenging for me to make connections sometimes, so I'm glad to know that it's possible for me to make new and lasting friendships.

I occasionally hike and swim and enjoy going for walks. For me, exercising has been more than just about getting physically fit. It's about opening a door to unforeseen things and finding new opportunities. I didn't know I was going to make new friends. I didn't know I was going to get inspired to do activities such as Spartan relays, half marathons, a mini triathlon and a historical Elvis Presley run in Nashville during the summer of 2015. And because I exercise regularly, I've inspired my son to join me at the gym to play basketball sometimes or to even lift weights together.

The point I'm making is that it is rewarding to join something you enjoy doing or want to try. It doesn't have to be a sport and you don't have to be good at it. When I first joined boot camp, I started out with little 5 lb dumbbells for several months and I could hardly do any sit-ups without complaining that my neck hurt. Perhaps you are interested in guitar lessons, yoga, drawing classes, or board game nights. Or maybe like me, you'd like to go back to one of your earlier passions that got lost over the years; for me, this is writing. When I rediscovered writing I felt like I found a piece of my true former self. You just never know what will come out of trying a new activity in terms of the connections you make with others (and yourself!)

In addition to exercising, I continue to work with counsellors, read a lot, meditate, talk to my friends about my journey, and play an active role in helping others who are going through confusing times. I've started a Meetup group for Adult Survivors of Childhood Abuse and Practical Healing which I host about once a month. We're a community of compassionate individuals who share a common past and we talk about our challenges and successes. I've also spoken at Mental Health Conferences in Vancouver and Ottawa where I shared my personal experiences with mental health and how we can reduce the stigma around it. And finally, I often journal, jotting down random thoughts, ideas, and inspiring things I've heard. I also blog about these things on my website called *Solace (www. solaceinnerhealth.com)* which is a site dedicated to our inner health. Otherwise, like many of us, life continues to truck along with my work, household chores, and routine errands that I am able to do now with a lighter step.

I am very happy with my life. There are so many things I am blessed with and I don't even have to look very far to appreciate those things. I am excited to see what the rest of my life will look like. In the meantime, I remain focused on the present and enjoy all the daily activities I do, which includes being a great dad to my amazing son.

I am fortunate to have many wonderful friends who I enjoy spending time with. I enjoy camping, playing board games, watching movies, going for a beer with them, and just getting together to catch up on life. My friends respect me for who I am and they are supportive of my journey. I no longer feel judged since discovering my own self-worth and it's been such a liberating feeling. Their kindness towards me reminds me how fortunate I am to have known them for all these years. Although we don't see each other as often as before, our relationship feels strong every time we do meet up. Ironically, I sometimes feel that our connection feels stronger with the time apart.

My sensitivity to feeling judged has been an issue for me over the years, especially when meeting new people. In the past, I subconsciously needed to gain acceptance from others because I lacked self-worth. What I've learned is that when someone is rude to me, their words or behaviour are not a reflection of who I am, but a reflection of themselves.

There's a dragon living inside all of us. It represents the suffering from our past. I once feared the dragon inside me and it was larger than life. I fed it with my insecurities and negative cognitions and it spat fire in the form of anger and shame towards others. But now the dragon inside me lives peacefully and is a welcomed friend. It will always be a part of me but now I have learned to accept it and look after it with love and self-compassion.

I feel that I've been very fortunate in life. Despite the hardships I faced growing up and as an adult, there was a greater purpose in all that happened in my life. I believe *there's a greater good to be learned on our journeys, otherwise life would be too predictable and I'm not willing to accept that.* I believe the unfortunate abuse I endured as a child and inflicted on others as an adult taught me lessons and provided me with a gift. The gift is the opportunity to inspire others who have gone through similar challenges to re-evaluate and re-shape their lives in a positive direction.

Your life is undoubtedly different than mine and your journey moving forward will be as well. If things are not easy for you and you feel as though you are carrying a heavy burden, then honour those thoughts and let them rise and fall. Allow them to flow in and out of you ever so peacefully. It's extremely easy to look at others and their faults and blame them for your problems and fears. However, you will only liberate yourself when you overcome your negative perspective. When you take ownership of your life and do the work in healing, you will feel taller and lighter and happiness will come when you least expect it. It's a beautiful feeling to meet the true "you" when you begin to process and unravel the past in a healthy way.

I hope you have found some insight and inspiration in my stories. There is no rule of thumb to healing except inner desire. When you are feeling frustrated with your own life and can amass enough bravery and courage to be vulnerable to look at yourself, change can happen. And you will want that change every day; it keeps fueling itself and eventually gets easier. Whenever you make mistakes, forgive yourself and remember that you'll have many opportunities to practice using the tools you've learned and to try again. My counsellor, Anita, once said to me with a smile of optimism, "It's a long life."

Take the time to do good things for yourself because you are worth it. Honour yourself with love and care, and recognize the greatness that you are. Take a bath, listen to some music, go for a walk, admire your garden, play with your kids, take your partner out for ice cream, or enjoy an evening out; cherish the good things in life.

Tomorrow will bring about a new day and new opportunities for growth. And it's only just beginning.

APPENDIX 1

Practical Healing Tools

We have thousands of thoughts running through our minds daily and things can get messy up there sometimes, especially for me. Here are some tools I learned over the years and I use them when I feel overwhelmed, stressed, anxious, or just need to slow things down. Use any one individually or a combination of them. These are tools you can learn from the recommended books listed in Appendix 2. Some of these tools are easier than others, but like most things, it takes practice and patience to learn how to use them effectively.

SHIFTING THOUGHTS (from COGNITIVE BEHAVIOUR THERAPY) – I USE THIS TECHNIQUE WHEN I FEEL ANXIOUS, STRESSED, or DEPRESSED.

- **Analyse an event** without judgement. Simply state the facts (For example: it's raining outside.)
- **Identify the thoughts** related to the event and consider how your feelings might be different depending on your thoughts. (For example: I can either choose to think that rainy days are miserable or I can choose to think that the rain will help me water my lawn.)
- **Identify your feelings**. Based on the two choices from my thoughts I might feel either depressed or content, respectively.
- **Take action on your behaviour**. If I feel depressed I might mope around the house. If I feel content, I might want to go out and watch a movie.
- The key thing is to be aware of when your thoughts are flooding in. This is the fork in the road when you can choose how you want to think.

BREATHING (FOUR SECOND HOLD) – I USE THIS WHEN I FEEL ANXIOUS, DEPRESSED, LONELY, or STRESSED.

- Sit quietly and comfortably and close your eyes
- Inhale deeply through your nose for four seconds, filling your lungs
- Hold it there for four seconds
- Exhale all the air through your mouth over four seconds
- Hold it there for four seconds

- Repeat at least four or five times (I usually try to do this up to ten times)

MEDITATION (MINDFULNESS AND BEING PRESENT) – I USE THIS WHEN I FEEL ANXIOUS, DEPRESSED, LONELY, or STRESSED.

- Sit quietly and comfortably close your eyes.
- Centre yourself to your breath and pay attention to the surrounding sounds.
- Pay attention to any discomfort or changes in any parts of your body. Paying attention to the body is important because it's an early warning sign to an onset of some potentially unhealthy thoughts (For example: increased heart rate, feeling warmer, tightness in temples and jaws). Simply recognize and acknowledge the body and focus on the discomfort. Allow those feelings to flow in and out of your mind like waves on a beach.
- Notice any thoughts and ideas running through your mind and re-centre yourself to your breathing. Simply slow down and acknowledge those thoughts and let them flow out of your mind.
- Continue being mindful to the present moment. You will eventually gain more self-awareness, clarity and relief.

LISTEN, EMPATHIZE, AND PARAPHRASE – I USE THIS WHEN I'M TRYING TO DIFFUSE AN ARGUMENT OR DISCUSSION.

- Listen to the other person's perspective with no interruptions and no attempts to think of your rebuttal (it's hard, I know!)

- Empathize. By stating how that person must be feeling, you acknowledge their hurt and frustration.
- Paraphrase. By reciting what the person just said, you validate them which means you've heard them. Validation is a powerful tool for changing a tense situation into one that's more amicable.
- After these three steps, hopefully you will have your turn to communicate and express your hurt and frustration in a healthy way.

KIND FATHER (from the book *"Becoming the Kind Father"* by Calvin Sandborn) – I USE THIS WHEN I FEEL DEPRESSED, ANXIOUS, or DISAPPOINTED WITH MYSELF.

- Use self-talk to bring compassion to yourself and cut yourself a break. It can do wonders to remind you that things are okay and you don't need to beat yourself up emotionally the way your care-givers may have.

DRAW LINES TO CONNECT PAST TO PRESENT AND UNDERSTAND THE TRUE HURT – I USE THIS WHEN I FEEL UPSET ABOUT LIFE IN GENERAL.

- Think of some of your hurts or triggers and how they connect to an incident or series of events while growing up.
- Understand the connections without blame and get to know yourself.
- You might find it to be amazing and uncanny, as I did, when you find the connections.

TIME OUT – I USE THIS WHEN I FEEL OVERWHELMED, or ANGRY.

- Respectfully let others know when you need time alone.

WATER – I DRINK SOME WHEN I FEEL ANGRY, TIRED, or STRESSED.

- Drink a cool glass of water – it's always good for you!

IDENTIFY TRUE FEELINGS - I USE THIS WHEN I FEEL ANGRY.

Instead of reacting to anger by lashing out, take time to consider what feelings might be underlying your anger. Perhaps these are feelings of:

- Hurt
- Anxiety/Nervousness
- Embarrassment
- Frustration
- Disappointment
- Pain
- Sadness
- Shock/Being stunned
- Curiosity
- Fear/Being frightened
- Jealousy
- Regret
- Loneliness

All of these are gentler and less aggressive emotions than anger. Once you've identified them, use the breathing or meditation tools to help you manage them.

APPENDIX 2

Recommended Books

Bradshaw, John. *Healing the Shame that Binds You.* Florida: Health Communications, Inc., 2005.

Bradshaw, John. *Homecoming: Reclaiming and Healing Your Inner Child.* New York: Bantam Books, 1992.

Brantley, Jeffrey. *Calming your Anxious Mind: How Mindfulness and Compassion can free you from Anxiety, Fear and Panic.* 2nd ed. California: New Harbinger Publications, Inc., 2007.

Brown, Brené. *The Gifts of Imperfection: Let Go of Who You Think You're Supposed to be and Embrace Who You Are, Your Guide to a Wholehearted Life.* Minnesota: Hazelden Publishing, 2010.

Engel, Beverly. *It Wasn't your Fault: Freeing Yourself from the Shame of Child Abuse with the Power of Self-Compassion.* California: New Harbinger Publications, Inc., 2015.

Engel, Beverly. *The Emotionally Abusive Relationship: How to Stop Being Abused and How to Stop Abusing, a Breakthrough Program to Overcome Unhealthy Patterns.* New Jersey: John Wiley & Sons, Inc., 2002.

Germer, Christopher K. *The Mindful Path to Self-Compassion: Freeing Yourself from Destructive Thoughts and Emotions.* New York: Guilford Press, 2009.

Izzo, John. *The Five Thieves of Happiness.* California: Berrett-Koehler Publishers, Inc., 2017.

Jampolsky, Gerald G. *Love is Letting go of Fear.* 3rd ed. New York: Celestial Arts, 2011.

Martin, Brian F. *Invincible: The 10 Lies You Learn Growing Up with Domestic Violence, and the Truths to Set You Free.* New York: Perigree Press, 2014.

Parnell, Laurel. *Tapping in: A Step-by-step Guide to Activating your Healing Resources through Bilateral Stimulation.* Colorado: Sounds True, Inc., 2008.

Reedy, Brad M. *The Journey of the Heroic Parent: Your Child's Struggle and the Road Home.* New York: Regan Arts, 2016.

Sandborn, Calvin. *Becoming the Kind Father: A Son's Journey.* British Columbia: New Society Publishers, 2007.

Shapiro, Francine. *Getting Past Your Past: Take Control of your Life with Self-help Techniques from EMDR Therapy.* New York: Rodale, Inc., 2012.

Williams, Mark, John Teasdale, Zindel Segal, and Jon Kabat-Zinn. *The Mindful Way Through Depression: Freeing yourself from Chronic Unhappiness.* New York: Guilford Press, 2007.

About The Author

Jason Lee was born in Vancouver, British Columbia in 1973. In 1980, he and his family moved to North Burnaby where he spent the rest of his childhood years. He grew up in a working-class home with parents, Anthony and Mary Lee, older brother, Joseph, and sister, Jacqueline.

Jason enjoys travelling. He has been fortunate enough to travel to many places in the world, including parts of Europe and the United States. He enjoys spending his time in Oregon and aspires to someday live along the coast of Cannon Beach. He's also been across Canada, visiting almost every province in his beautiful country. He hopes to someday travel to Asia. In particular, he'd like to travel to Japan with his son, Josh, and eat endless bowls of ramen together.

Jason has a love for animals - especially cats, rabbits, and hamsters - and has a soft spot for Josh's two bunnies, Connie and Baxter. He recently adopted a beautiful cat from Bellingham, WA and named her Inori which means "prayer" in Japanese.

During his free time he enjoys going to the gym, swimming, watching movies, writing, live theatre, spending time with friends, hiking, gaming, camping, watching hockey, and playing basketball.

Jason has created a website called *"Solace"* *(www.solace-innerhealth.com)* where he's a lifestyle blogger on taking care of your inner health and reducing the stigma around mental illness. His rediscovery of writing takes him back to his days in elementary school and to creative writing which were his favourite classes in school.

Jason is also a Speaker, Certified Life Coach, Group Facilitator, and Collaborator specializing in Childhood Abuse, Bullying, Emotional Abuse, and Mental Health. His lived experience provides him with deep insight and knowledge to skillfully help people who want to take the next steps towards healing. Jason has helped others move forward from their challenges and to learn how to take accountability for their lives. He is compassionate with his approach and driven to inspire and empower people to see their true potential.

For more information and opportunities to work with Jason, contact him at *livingwiththedragon@gmail.com* and visit him at *www.solaceinnerhealth.com.*

Testimonials

"In his first book, Jason Lee invites men to walk the path of transformation. Full of relatable experiences, this book is a must read for men who want a sunnier future for themselves and their families." - Guillermo Comesaña, M.Ed., R.C.C.

"Jason's book is a personal story of one man's healing journey from childhood abuse and years of accumulated shame from societal and cultural influences. It is an inspirational mix of personal reflections about his life, and suggestions for healing, growth and change. The book should be read slowly, absorbed and used as a healing tool, as each chapter contains hidden gems of wisdom, that can only come from the hard work of personal growth. I recommend Living with the Dragon as an inspirational and motivating resource." - Anita Bloy, R.C.C.

Notes
(Endnotes)

1   Sarah Boesveld, "One-third of Canadians have suffered child abuse, highest rates in the western provinces, study says," National Post, posted April 22, 2014, http://nationalpost.com/g00/news/canada/one-third-of-canadians-have-suffered-child-abuse-highest-rates-in-the-western-provinces-study-says/wcm/db62011c-831b-419e-80c0-504d17c3e9b4?i10c.referrer=.

2   Calvin Sandborn, Becoming the Kind Father: A Son's Journey (British Columbia: New Society Publishers, 2007), 24-26.

3   Beverly Engel, It Wasn't Your Fault: Freeing Yourself from the Shame of Childhood Abuse with the Power of Self-Compassion (California: New Harbinger Publications, Inc., 2015).

4   Brian F. Martin, Invincible: The 10 Lies You Learn Growing Up with Domestic Violence, and the Truths to Set You Free (New York: The Perigree Press, 2014), 44.

5   Laura Petherbridge, "12 Traits of an Abusive Relationship," Crosswalk, last modified July 30, 2009, http://www.crosswalk.com/family/marriage/12-traits-of-an-abusive-relationship-11606848.html.

6   Beverly Engel, It Wasn't Your Fault: Freeing Yourself from the Shame of Childhood Abuse with the Power of Self-Compassion (California: New Harbinger Publications, Inc., 2015).

7   "Schizophrenia," adapted from "Schizophrenia: A Guide for People with Schizophrenia and Their Families," Centre for Addiction and Mental Health, © 1999, http://www.camh.ca/en/hospital/health_information/a_z_mental_health_and_addiction_information/schizophrenia/Pages/Schizophrenia.aspx.

8   "Mental Disorders Affect One in Four People," WHO.int, posted October 4, 2001, http://www.who.int/whr/2001/media_centre/press_release/en/.

9   "Mental Health – Depression," Health Canada, last modified February 9, 2009, https://www.canada.ca/en/health-canada/services/healthy-living/your-health/diseases/mental-health-depression.html.

10 Merriam-Webster, s.v. "validate," accessed July 2, 2017, https://www.merriam-webster.com/dictionary/validate.

11 For the sake of confidentiality, I've used fictional names and left several details out.

12   Merriam-Webster, s.v. "tradition," accessed July 3, 2017, https://www.merriam-webster.com/dictionary/tradition.

LIVING WITH THE DRAGON

CPSIA information can be obtained
at www.ICGtesting.com
Printed in the USA
LVOW12s0420171017

552673LV00001B/4/P